DUST
&GLORY

Text copyright © David Runcorn 2015
The author asserts the moral right to be identified as the author of this work

Published by
The Bible Reading Fellowship
15 The Chambers, Vineyard
Abingdon OX14 3FE
United Kingdom
Tel: +44 (0)1865 319700
Email: enquiries@brf.org.uk
Website: www.brf.org.uk
BRF is a Registered Charity

ISBN 978 0 85746 357 9

First published 2015
10 9 8 7 6 5 4 3 2 1
All rights reserved

Acknowledgements
Unless otherwise stated, scripture quotations are taken from The New Revised
Standard Version of the Bible, Anglicised edition, copyright © 1989, 1995 by the
Division of Christian Education of the National Council of the Churches of Christ
in the United States of America. Used by permission. All rights reserved.

Scripture taken from THE MESSAGE. Copyright © 1993, 1994, 1995, 1996, 2000,
2001, 2002. Used by permission of NavPress Publishing Group.

Scripture quotations taken from The Holy Bible, New International Version
(Anglicised edition) copyright © 1979, 1984, 2011 by Biblica. Used by permission
of Hodder & Stoughton Publishers, an Hachette UK company. All rights reserved.
'NIV' is a registered trademark of Biblica. UK trademark number 1448790.

Cover photo: mycola/Thinkstock

Every effort has been made to trace and contact copyright owners for material
used in this resource. We apologise for any inadvertent omissions or errors, and
would ask those concerned to contact us so that full acknowledgement can be
made in the future.

A catalogue record for this book is available from the British Library

Printed and bound by CPI Group (UK) Ltd, Croydon CR0 4YY

DUST
&GLORY

DAILY BIBLE READINGS FROM
ASH WEDNESDAY TO EASTER DAY

DAVID RUNCORN

To
Simon Kingston
friend, critic and fellow pilgrim
in gratitude

CONTENTS

WEEK 4: HIDDEN AND REVEALED

WEEK 5: HABITS, REFLEXES AND RESPONSES

WEEK 6: IN THE SHADOW OF THE CROSS

MAKING SPACE TO GROW

We do not grow by accident, and growing rarely happens in ideal circumstances. Nor is the task ever completed. Life is always a becoming. Growing requires a continual willingness to adapt, the capacity to make do and the imagination to improvise. There is also the constant challenge of being reconciled to what we would *not* have chosen in the life we find ourselves living. Our most significant growing is probably what happens while we are making other plans. Learning to respond and manage our choices and dilemmas fruitfully, we call 'maturity' and the Bible calls 'wisdom'.

Growing needs time. It is not for hurrying. Growing is about something far more important than accumulating skills and knowledge. If life is to flourish in security and truth, it needs wisdom, which can be called a way of *slow* knowing. Contemporary life has no patience with slowness. If nothing else, it delays us, and what is the point of that? We have made speed a priority and have made a technology of information. We presume 'knowing' to be a right and we wield knowledge as a means to power—but do we know our perils? 'We are now far too clever to survive without wisdom,' wrote the pioneering economist E.F. Schumacher. The present global ecological crisis has been well described as 'a crisis of knowledge without wisdom'.[1]

The ancient Christian communities knew that the task of growing in the faith and life of Christ was searching and profound. It needs more than good intentions. One of their initiatives was to set aside a special period of prayer, self-examination and teaching for new followers who were preparing for their baptism on Easter Day. Over time, the value of this season became so apparent that it came to be commended to everyone in the church. This is the origin of the season of Lent. It is one of three 40-day periods in the church's year, the others being Advent (leading up to Christmas) and Easter (leading *from* the resurrection).

The name itself, 'Lent', comes from an ancient word meaning 'spring' or 'long', referring to that time in the year (in Western Europe) when the days are beginning to lengthen and the world is turning from the death of winter towards the warmth and promise of summer.

So this is a book to accompany the work of turning— the journey from death to life. It is not a how-to book. I hope it will feel more like a conversation. Its themes range across the whole business of living and believing. The daily reflections tend to explore questions rather than give answers, and at times you may well want to argue or protest. There are suggestions for the necessary self-examination and heart-searching that growing requires. Some chapters were unsettling and disturbing to write, as they must be if we are to seek authentic faith in a world like ours. At other times I hope you will be caught out by joy, surprised by laughter and stirred to curiosity and wonder. Growing into faithful living never happens without vulnerability: I hope you will also find sources of healing, mercy and rest in these pages, for whenever you may need them.

Just one feature of the book may need explanation. Books

that accompany this season stop at Easter, so they tend to miss out the resurrection. But risen life needs just as much discipline, nurture and attention as sin and penitence—perhaps more—and, while these qualities are lacking, it is perhaps not surprising if perceptions of Christian believing are closer to joyless denial than to the surprise of risen life. So, on each of the five Sundays (which is Resurrection Day), the focus in this book is on Easter and the risen life.

Please journey with the book at the pace you find helpful. No one will come checking if you take your own route and time across these days. But please, as a general rule, read more slowly than you normally do, and linger longer with what you find. It is the slow knowing that we need most. There is no hurry.

ASH WEDNESDAY
TO SATURDAY

WONDER

O Lord, our Sovereign,
how majestic is your name in all the earth!
You have set your glory above the heavens…
When I look at your heavens, the work of your fingers,
the moon and the stars that you have established,
what are human beings that you are mindful of them…?
Yet you have made them a little lower than God,
and crowned them with glory and honour…
you have put all things under their feet…
O Lord, our Sovereign,
how majestic is your name in all the earth!

PSALM 8:1, 3–6, 9

Picture a park on a warm summer afternoon. A couple have enjoyed a picnic and are dozing contentedly on the grass, unaware that a camera is hovering just above them. But we are looking through the camera.

At an unseen signal, it begins to rise vertically into the sky. The couple, the park, the neighbourhood and the city successively shrink into the distance. Before long, we have left planet earth altogether and are travelling deeper and deeper into space. Planets, stars and galaxies slide past as the camera continues out to the farthest reaches of the cosmos.

There in utter darkness the camera pauses for a moment before going into reverse. We begin a silent return across the vast tracts of the universe, back to earth and down, towards the city, the park, the sleeping couple and the remains of the picnic, where it all began.

But the camera doesn't stop there. When it reaches the couple, it continues its descent, right into the body of one of the sleepers. Moving through the blood vessels, membranes and cells, in ever finer detail, it reaches the micro-particles that lie at the source of human life as we know it.

Meanwhile, the couple on the picnic rug are completely unaware of it all. They are asleep.[2]

Being asleep, sleepwalking through life, is a common diagnosis that the ancient spiritual traditions offer for our human condition. 'Most people, even though they don't know it, are asleep. They're born asleep, they live asleep, they marry in their sleep, they breed children in their sleep, they die in their sleep without ever waking up. They never understand the loveliness and the beauty of this thing that we call human existence.' (Anthony de Mello)[3]

The awakening we need is not to some notion of usefulness, achievement or productivity. It is simply to a wondering, which is already there within us, but buried deep. This awakening transformed the faith of the writer G.K. Chesterton—the discovery that 'at the back of our brains, so to speak, there was a forgotten blaze or burst of astonishment at our existence.' (G.K. Chesterton)[4]

People in early Christian icons are painted in the sort of proportions often found in children's drawings. Their eyes are saucer-wide, expressions fixed in astonishment at what they have been awakened to. Their mouths are very small but the ears are painted large. The message is clear: watch, listen, wonder—and be slow to speak. This is not the time for chat or speculation.

How does such awakening come? We sometimes speak of a 'wake-up call'—a moment in life that jolts and shocks us into new awareness. It may come in the encounter with a new culture or landscape that a holiday brings. We see the world in a new way, in a new light. The birth of a child often sparks an awakening of profound wonder. It is not uncommon for couples with little previous interest in spiritual life to awaken suddenly to a need and longing. The feeling can surface when life is under threat. Emerging from the shadow of a serious cancer scare, a friend writes of an awakened wonder in the ordinary things of life: 'Things we take for granted, like having a shower, drinking orange juice, have an extraordinary brilliancy at the moment.'

I recall a time of personal exhaustion. Burned out on life, church and God, I booked a day at a monastery. Beyond thought, prayer or sleep, I simply sat in the garden for hours, staring at a small patch of grass between my feet. Nothing dramatic happened. I could not have coped if it had. But I remember, very slowly, beginning to notice just how much life there was in that grass—its shifting colour and texture in the sun, the dew, the tiny insects... and I began to awaken again to life.

Wonder, like reverence, is not for grasping to suit our own ends or needs. It requires a certain surrender, a self-forgetting. It is about paying attention to what is already present but too easily unnoticed. It takes practice, but it is all there waiting for me: 'When I look...'

FOR REFLECTION

Choose something, anything—and for a few minutes simply give your undivided attention to it.

LONGING

As a deer longs for flowing streams,
so my soul longs for you, O God.
My soul thirsts for God,
for the living God.
When shall I come and behold
the face of God?
My tears have been my food…
while people say to me continually,
'Where is your God?'…

Why are you cast down, O my soul,
and why are you disquieted within me?
Hope in God; for I shall again praise him.

PSALM 42:1–3, 11

We are not by the leafy lakeside of an English country park here. A deer stands still in the heat of the day. Nostrils are lifted, quivering and straining for any hint of water on the parched breeze. Deer can scent water from up to five miles away, which is just as well. In this wilderness, thirst is a matter of life and death—and for this psalm writer the search for God is just that. Something has gone missing that he knows his life depends on.

Our most significant growing in life can often be traced to the experience of loss. Sometimes it is the impact of a particular event—a tragedy, perhaps. In the pain, in need of meaning and comfort, we find that answers that have worked for us until this point now sound hopelessly simplistic or even wrong. We must go searching with our questions, without yet knowing if we will find what we need to sustain life and faith.

Sometimes, without warning or reason, life that has been fulfilling just goes empty on us. Weariness descends. An activity that once contained degrees of meaning and security no longer does so. We are bored with what so recently stimulated. The music no longer excites. The words have emptied of meaning. Where has it all gone? Why am I downcast? How should I respond?

That seems to be the story behind this psalm. The excitement of faith has gone and the poet is missing it acutely. He feels mocked by others because he can no longer join in as he once did. Anyone who finds themselves on the edge of faith while in the midst of enthusiastic believers knows how that feels.

He cries out to God, who has vanished. He also talks in perplexity to his own soul. He doesn't know himself any more. 'Why am I feeling like this?' At such times it is easy to assume that the fault lies with us (and there are times when it may do), but notice that the poet does not make that assumption here.

When a crisis hit me, some years ago, I was on the edge of a breakdown and felt I was losing everything. The faith that had been with me for a lifetime offered no solace. In fact, it was part of the problem. I remember saying to my counsellor, 'I don't think I believe this any more.' The response was so wise: 'You do not look to me like someone who has lost their faith. But you are living out of a part of yourself that you have not spent much time with before. So it is not surprising if you are feeling like a stranger to yourself.'

Our longings are always the starting place. They trace the contours of our desires. They map our dreams. They reveal our personal geography, so they are vocational in shape. Qualifications and questions that ask for 'yes' or 'no' answers are not of use here; nor is the interviewer's question, 'Do you think you have the skills and experience needed?' or, if the focus is religious, 'Do you believe God has called you?' There is a wiser question, still asked in monastic life at times of choice-making and commitment: 'What is your desire?' *This 'desire' is not the same as selfish desire.* It is a way of speaking about my most authentic self, the 'real me', as God has made me. The question is asked only after a long and careful discernment.

We must stay with the longing. Instead of trying to 'solve' it by searching for excitement, we must listen to it carefully. Monastic life has a saying for such times: 'Stay in your cell and your cell will teach you everything.' Of course, that is the last thing we want to do, but the answer to this restiveness is not distraction. The longing is the prayer, so pray it with all your heart.

A feature of those psalms that begin with distress and loss is that they often finish with praise. But 'happy ending' faith is not on offer here. The willingness to long, to thirst, to stay with the emptiness and the questions, brings its gift. The psalmist knows this.

So we wait in hope—for our longing is the clearest sign that what we seek is already to be found in us.

FOR REFLECTION

What is my desire?

SHUTTING THE DOOR

'Whenever you pray, do not be like the hypocrites; for they love to stand and pray in the synagogues and at the street corners, so that they may be seen by others. Truly I tell you, they have received their reward. But whenever you pray, go into your room and shut the door and pray to your Father who is in secret; and your Father who sees in secret will reward you.

When you are praying, do not heap up empty phrases as the Gentiles do; for they think that they will be heard because of their many words. Do not be like them, for your Father knows what you need before you ask him.

MATTHEW 6:5–8

'Standing', 'being seen', 'on street corners'—in that time and culture it must have all looked very pious and spiritual or they would not have been doing it, but the reality was quite different. 'Hypocrisy' is play-acting, pretending to an image that has no reality. As an Oxford professor once said of a colleague, 'On the surface, he's profound, but deep down, he's superficial.' What concerns Jesus about hypocrites is their utter preoccupation with image—what others are seeing and thinking—under the cloak of prayer and devotion. Of course, none of their play-acting requires God to be real or present. In fact, there is no serious interest in God here at all. This kind of religion is functionally atheist.

For his own followers, Jesus sets up a contrast between public and secret activity—between behaviour aimed at impressing and achieving reputation from those around us and behaviour known and seen by God alone, who is also in secret. He is *not* saying, 'Do not express your faith openly.' Christian faith is unashamedly public faith: we are called to be a light to the world (Matthew 5:14). But Jesus plainly believes that this vocation comes with a severe health warning. Perhaps these words reflect the discipline and focus that Jesus himself had to learn in his life in this world.

How do we apply his words to faith today? Is this kind of hypocrisy really a hazard that we face, or can we assume Jesus is aiming just at Pharisees, and perhaps television evangelists, and breathe a sigh of relief? In fact, the church in our time is under severe pressure to find ways of being more visible, more public. If so, then public faith still has its perils, and Jesus' warning may be very timely. Not everything is for telling.

The church has a secret to keep. Christian faith is rooted in a source of life, of being known and recognised, that is out of sight. On the surface, the pressures on the church to change and grow in these difficult times feel very urgent. The longing to achieve change and growth may be genuine and faithful, but in such times it is perilously easy to be driven by what is visible. Everything becomes defined by its useful-ness for public impact. We can be seduced by demands for relevance and a preoccupation with measurable outcomes. Buildings and forms of worship are designed for maximum accessibility for outsiders. We anxiously rehearse what we want to say to each other, but we are in danger of losing any sense of God 'who is in secret'.

What do you hear in all this? Where do the challenges lie? For Jesus, there is a vital line between public faith and the secret place. He is quite uncompromising. The very desire to possess for ourselves or to be seen by others disqualifies us: we become inauthentic. Even to want our faith to be *visible* disqualifies us. We must have an intentional focus on God alone and on whatever he wills to bless.

So what are you like at trusting in secret? It means going out of sight. It requires a willingness to lose control of outcomes. It means trusting to the one who is unseen the secret of who we may become. The ancient teachers of faith have always taught that the marketplace is a hazardous place for those who have not learned to be alone.

'So,' says Jesus, 'when you pray, shut the door.'

'OK, it is shut. What now?'

'Shut the door.'

'No prayer tips or techniques, Jesus?'

'Just shut the door.'

'No workshops on finding stillness, on posture, on breathing? Or a seminar on work/life balance, perhaps?'

'Just shut the door!'

Jesus teaches very little on how to pray except that we should keep it short! His concern is with our core motivation—with the heart. He calls this 'shutting the door'.

There in secret, the one who is in secret—the hidden Father—waits for us. We won't need to pile up the words. He already knows.

FOR REFLECTION

Just shut the door!

ONE THING NECESSARY

Now as they went on their way, he entered a certain village, where a woman named Martha welcomed him into her home. She had a sister named Mary, who sat at the Lord's feet and listened to what he was saying. But Martha was distracted by her many tasks; so she came to him and asked, 'Lord, do you not care that my sister has left me to do all the work by myself? Tell her then to help me.' But the Lord answered her, 'Martha, Martha, you are worried and distracted by many things; there is need of only one thing. Mary has chosen the better part, which will not be taken away from her.'
LUKE 10:38–42

Martha usually comes off badly in the telling of this story. It is assumed to be teaching the importance of the 'higher' contemplative calling compared with the busy activist world of daily life—and the story can read like that. Martha is rushing around while Mary is still and silent. Martha is stressed; Mary is calm. Martha is rebuked by Jesus; Mary is praised.

But the story needs Martha. It only takes place because of her: it begins with her initiative to welcome Jesus into their house. (This may have been Jesus' first meeting with a family to whom he grew very close, and their home was one where he spent a lot of time.) Martha is not condemned for being busy. There is nothing wrong with being busy, and any life worth living will have its share of stresses. Jesus responds to Martha with concern, not judgement. He is more attentive to her than to Mary, in fact. There is tenderness in the repetition of her name (v. 41). He recognises that she is 'worried and distracted over many things'. Dis-tracted literally means 'pulled apart'.

Mary presents a sharp contrast to Martha. Though not to be viewed as an idealised model of contemplative life, she does have an enviable capacity for sitting still while others around her are winding themselves up. Which character do you most easily identity with? There are always responses that come naturally to us, while we struggle with others. But differences are not deficiencies.

Mary's stillness was not meek or submissive. *She* chose her place there—as a disciple, at the feet of a rabbi, being taught. This was not a woman's place in that society and would have scandalised others who were present. What made her determined to walk in and sit in front of Jesus, we do not know. She would have needed a defiant toughness to see it through. Jesus' support for her makes clear that there had been demands to remove her from the room: her choice 'will not be taken away from her' (v. 42).

Mary and Martha need each other, for all their tensions. It takes the faith of both characters to tell this story, and the relationship between them is one that we all have to work at. It is Martha who welcomes Jesus into a life that, like ours, is easily overwhelmed and distracted, losing sight of priorities. Mary models a subversive response. In the midst of endless tasks and urgent demands, she just sits down and will not be moved—and a choice that is often called thoughtless and selfish, Jesus calls 'the better part'.

There is an ancient method of practising stillness in the midst of the distractions of life. It is a way of praying based on the simple, continuous repetition of a word or phrase, such as 'Come, Lord', 'My rock' or 'Love'. This is sometimes called an 'anchor word' because we drop it like an anchor below the surface of our storm-tossed lives. There in the depths, it anchors us on to the rock that is Christ. Our task is to repeat it quietly, perhaps on the rhythm of our breathing, until the surface of life begins to reflect the deeper security in which it is held. Just try it. It is not to be measured by how it feels or whether it is 'working', or even whether it is 'making sense' to us. For many in a world like ours, it is the 'one thing necessary'. As this prayer takes a hold, over time, it has a way of pulling in all the distracted strands of our lives until they begin to fulfil their one true purpose—to attend to the presence of Jesus.

Today is a busy day for me. The usual demands are pressing. The first thing necessary is to go and stand at the door of my life and welcome Jesus into it. Now one thing still remains. Defying all the protests that there is too much to do, I will sit down here, in the presence of Jesus, and refuse to budge.

PRAYER

Lord, help me to balance the relationship between being busy *for* you and sitting still *with* you.

WEEK 1

BECOMING WHO I AM

DO NOT BE AFRAID

Very early on the first day of the week, when the sun had risen, they went to the tomb... As they entered the tomb, they saw a young man, dressed in a white robe, sitting on the right side; and they were alarmed. But he said to them, 'Do not be alarmed; you are looking for Jesus of Nazareth, who was crucified. He has been raised; he is not here. Look, there is the place they laid him. But go, tell his disciples and Peter that he is going ahead of you...' So they went out and fled from the tomb, for terror and amazement had seized them; and they said nothing to anyone, for they were afraid.

MARK 16:2, 5–8

Mark spares no one in his reporting of the discovery of the resurrection of Jesus. They came, saw, listened—and fled in terror. 'Fear' and 'alarm' are also words scattered through these accounts. Whenever angels, or Jesus himself, appear to the disciples, they need a lot of calming: 'Do not be afraid' and 'Peace be with you'. So the earliest Gospel account we have ends on a note of overwhelming fear. The disciples simply ran away and told no one!

Should this surprise us? Or might we wonder how a faith based on such an event could ever have become so tame and predictable? 'Does anyone have the foggiest idea what sort of power we so blithely invoke?' asks writer Annie Dillard.[5] Not that fear is ever the basis of faith: terror is not a motivation for love.

I recall attending a Christian event at which dramatic manifestations of spiritual power began happening around me. I was afraid, but it was clear to me that something was going on that I wanted to call 'holy'. It was the presence of God. I also felt challenged by how little fear featured in my relationship with God. Religion can all too easily become a refined attempt to keep God 'safely' under control.

Early in C.S. Lewis's 'Narnia Chronicles' there is a moment when the children realise that Aslan, the mysterious presence whose coming all the faithful in Narnia long for, is a lion. 'Ooh, is he safe?' they ask, nervously. 'Safe? Who said anything about safe?' comes the reply. ''Course he's not safe. But he's good.'[6]

There is a kind of fear that is positively encouraged in the Bible, that we are urged to learn. 'The fear of the Lord is the beginning of wisdom' is a saying repeated often (see, for example, Proverbs 9:10). Fearing the Lord is what wise people do. It is not a cringing terror but an appropriate awe and reverence that gives life its true shape and priority. It finds beautiful expression in the lines from F. Faber's hymn, 'O how I fear thee, living God, with deepest, tend'rest fears'. This kind of fear is 'pure' and 'enduring', says the psalmist (Psalm 19:9, also translated 'clean'). It is a healthy fear that is actually good for us. It lays a secure, enduring foundation for living.

For the early disciples, those first journeys into risen life required the management of fear. We should not be surprised if they still do. It may be that the deepest fear on the threshold of the resurrection is the sheer scale of God. We suffer from a spiritual kind of agoraphobia. We fear the invitation and adventure of the wide, infinite spaciousness of divine love. Of course we do!

What place does fear have in your experiences of life and faith? Fear is at its most powerful when we are running from it. There must come a moment when we turn and face it, call it by name and listen to it. This takes courage and needs loving support. We may have good reason for the fears within us.

The language we use is important. When I say, 'I am afraid', it is not actually true. I mean that there is fear in me, but it is not a statement about the *whole* of me: 'I' am not afraid. This gives me some perspective. I need to listen to my fears but not let them take over.

The secret is this: there is a place behind my terrors, fears and anxieties where I am not afraid or anxious. It is my truest self, known and secure in the love of God. From there, as the grip of anxiety loosens, I may begin to listen to my fears and what they are telling me, and reach out to them in love.

This is precisely where the disciples find Jesus in those first resurrection encounters. It is where he meets us too. 'Peace… do not be afraid,' he says.

FOR REFLECTION

May my only fear be fear that is wise.

THE DESERTED PLACE

The apostles gathered around Jesus, and told him all that they had done and taught. He said to them, 'Come away to a deserted place all by yourselves and rest a while.' For many were coming and going, and they had no leisure even to eat. And they went away in the boat to a deserted place by themselves. Now many saw them going and recognised them, and they hurried there on foot from all the towns and arrived ahead of them.

MARK 6:30–33

The disciples are reporting back to the one who sent them. 'How did it go?' Anyone who has been part of team training exercises will recognise the importance of these spaces for feedback and reflection. Their work had been relentless. Sometimes it has to be like that; it can even be exhilarating for a time. But the cost is high if it remains unrelenting in the long term. In all too much contemporary living, this is now the way of life.

The main points in this story are emphasised by being mentioned twice.

■ *'Many'* sums up the schedule of activities from which they have just returned. It also describes the clamouring crowds that they are trying to get away from. The 'many' are always out there and they always seem to know exactly where to find us.

- 'Come *away*': Jesus knows they are exhausted and need to stop. They must get away. This is a regular feature of Jesus' own life, but it takes planning and even a degree of cunning that is curiously absent in this story.
- They need 'a *deserted* place'. I assume that someone whose teaching is so full of references to parties, banquets and celebrations would not be slow to organise the equivalent of team curry evenings or nights out with his disciples, but that is not the priority here. Geography matters. Deserted places are important precisely because they don't deal in excitements or distractions.
- All of this is so that his disciples will be '*by yourselves*'. The invitation from Jesus is not to be 'with me', as you might expect. The focus is not on God at all. They must be alone. (Leave the phones and tablets at home, too.)

There is a very practical wisdom at work here. Extra meetings, training programmes or seminars on work/life balance are not much use when people are simply tired and hungry. Sustainable rhythms of life do not emerge from chaotic diaries. There is a well-known story of a remote mountain expedition in which the heavily laden native porters refused all demands to travel faster and finally sat down in protest. Asked why, they explained that they had to stop to let their souls catch up with them.

We may not understand the wisdom and necessity of this until we just do it. What are you like when you are alone? Who are you when there is no one else to see you? What do you do when no one requires you to do anything? What is your relationship with yourself? Even communities need a way of being 'by themselves' that is not defined by their 'many' shared tasks and projects, however worthy. Until we are present to ourselves, there can be no meeting with anyone else, let alone God.

The BBC TV documentary *The Big Silence* traced the journey of five people through the experience of an eight-day silent retreat. Their only conversation was their daily meeting with a personal guide. Only one had any religious background; all came from very contemporary, highly driven lifestyles. As the silence deepened, they entered into a bare and arid place that they frequently described as 'wilderness' or 'desert'. Since there was no one else there, it was their own life they were experiencing. Away from all that crowded living, their first encounter was not with God; it was with themselves—and it felt like a desert. They had lived so long in busy, hectic activity that they could not be sure if any other way of living was possible. With wise guidance, their first task was to begin to be with themselves at a new depth.

Returning to Mark's Gospel, the attempt of the disciples to get away from it all completely fails. The crowds are there waiting for them. When choosing a desert, make sure it is deserted enough! We can perhaps find some comfort, though, in knowing that even Jesus' attempts at planning quiet days could go wrong at times.

Of course the crowds *always* arrive in the stillness. We cannot leave this world. The crowds are not the problem. We need another way of meeting them, no longer driven by urgency and surface needs, and for that we need the desert places.

It doesn't always work, but we will keep trying—and so will Jesus.

PRAYER

Lord, help me to find stillness, so that in my busyness I do
not leave my soul behind.

WHO ARE YOU?

This is the testimony given by John when the Jews sent priests and Levites from Jerusalem to ask him, 'Who are you?' He confessed and did not deny it, but confessed, 'I am not the Messiah.' And they asked him, 'What then? Are you Elijah?' He said, 'I am not.' 'Are you the prophet?' He answered, 'No.' Then they said to him, 'Who are you? Let us have an answer for those who sent us. What do you say about yourself?' He said, 'I am the voice of one crying out in the wilderness, "Make straight the way of the Lord"', as the prophet Isaiah said.

JOHN 1:19–23

As the sounds of the overture to John's Gospel fade away ('In the beginning was the Word...') the action begins with an abrupt question: 'Who are you?' It receives an even more abrupt reply.

Rumours have reached the authorities of a strange man out in the desert. He is drawing considerable crowds. His message is controversial, but no one knows who he is or where he is from. So they send out messengers to check his credentials. Religion does attract more than its share of people who like things ordered and authorised.

It is a terse exchange. The messengers keep trying to fit John into their own categories: 'Are you the Messiah? ... Are you Elijah?' His replies are brief and unambiguous.

A striking feature of this whole opening chapter is the number of negatives running through it. *'No'*, 'I did *not*', 'he was *not*', 'you do *not* know', '*not* of human will' and 'I am *not*' occur over twelve times. The message is clear: whatever is happening here is *not* for knowing on any familiar terms. Geographically, politically and theologically, this stranger and his message are outside all the usual categories and beyond the presumed centres of authority and power.

For John the Baptist, the beginning of life, ministry and vocation lies in knowing who he is *not*. He simply refuses to be known by the titles, expectations or projections of the world around him. He will not even enter the discussion on those terms. For him, these are the wrong questions to the wrong person. Here, two very different worlds never meet.

How would you answer the question 'Who are you?'

This does presuppose that we know the answer in the first place. The point at issue is where we find our identity and the measures by which we think we recognise ourselves. It also concerns how much we live in thrall to the demanding scripts of the world around us. The answer will probably include details such as my family, home, education, qualifications and career. My social networks and lifestyle will be included, and much else besides.

There is nothing wrong with any of these in themselves. The problem is the way we attach ourselves to them as a means of securing our 'I am' in the world—the way we define ourselves by them.

The pressures that shape the way we identify ourselves are powerful. Work consultant and writer David Whyte identifies this as a primary problem today. He describes a world driven by its insecurities into a kind of collective amnesia. 'The day may be full, we may be incredibly busy, but we have forgotten who is busy and why we are busy. Our lives take the form of an absence… We have to realise that our lives are at stake.'[7]

A gospel that starts with 'I am *not*' can easily be confused with judgemental religion, but we should consider the possibility that this 'not' is unexpectedly good news. What if another story really is on offer, another way of knowing ourselves—one that is not about earning or achieving, one in which I no longer have to sustain the effort of being in the centre, because I am *not*? In fact, in the stories of Jesus that will soon follow, it is precisely those who are *not*—those outside the social world of reputation and respectability and without any way of competing with it—who witness most vividly to the gift and joy of another way of living.

John's 'I am not' is first a call to repentance. I must turn from the places where, out of anxiety or ambition, I seek a name and security for myself. But always more important than what we turn from is what we turn to. For the moment, in these opening verses, there is apparently one among us whom 'we do not know' (v. 26).

So, with the crowds out there in wilderness, let the excitement and suspense build. The story is moving towards a revelation, and John is pointing towards him. This is all his work—and ours. 'Behold!'

PRAYER

Help me to know who I am not.

DUST THAT DREAMS

Bless the Lord, O my soul,
and all that is within me,
bless his holy name…
For he knows how we are made;
he remembers that we are dust.
As for mortals, their days are like grass;
they flourish like a flower of the field;
for the wind passes over it, and it is gone,
and its place knows it no more.
But the steadfast love of the Lord
is from everlasting to everlasting
on those who fear him.

PSALM 103:1, 14–18

'Remember that you are dust and to dust you shall return.'
As the words were spoken over me, a thumb firmly smeared
an oily mixture of ash and dirt on my forehead, making a
sign of the cross. It was Ash Wednesday and I had been to
church. On the way home from the service, I stopped for
some chips. The young shop assistant looked curiously at me
several times before her face suddenly lit up with recognition.
'Oh, you've been to church!' she exclaimed. My forehead!
I had forgotten. That morning at school she had learned
about Ash Wednesday—what ashing is, how it is done and

why Christians do it. Like many ancient faith communities, Christians use the ritual action of smearing or covering with dust and ashes to express visibly some core beliefs about human life and faith.

As I left with my chips, I caught my reflection in the shop window. It was a very large smudge.

What am I called to remember under this strange sign?

- Dust reminds me of my origins. The name of the first human being in the Bible, Adam, comes from the Hebrew *Adamah*, meaning 'earth'. I am formed from the dust of the earth. We now know what the psalmist did not, that the dust of earthly life is a gift of the entire universe. Every atom in my body was forged in the explosive furnaces of the farthest stars. This humbles me—but humility is not self-negation. True humility creates a space for wonder. I can learn from the rabbi who always carried two pieces of paper in his pockets: one told him he was dust and ashes; the other told him that for him the whole universe was made.

- Dust reminds me of my mortality. What began as dust will return to dust. Like the grass of the fields and flowers in my garden, my life is a brief, passing thing. It may be that our perennial capacity for messing up, our misguided priorities, our presumptions and assumptions about who we are, all lie in an unwillingness to live with this truth. This reminder brings me down to earth.

- Covering with dust was an ancient way of expressing penitence and sorrow for sin. Under this sign of dust I acknowledge my waywardness and wilfulness. I commit myself afresh to self-examination of life, motives, values and priorities. I repent of my sins.

Having done all this, I remain dust. What may I hope for? Who makes *anything* of dust? Only God: 'He knows... he remembers that we are but dust,' says the psalmist. This does not seem to frustrate God—quite the reverse. We inspire him, it seems! After all, he chose dust to be the prime ingredient for his crowning work in creation—a creature who bears his image. Shaped out of barren ground, the first creature of dust became a living being when God breathed into his nostrils (Genesis 2:7).

So here I am, a dust creature, yet alive in the very breath of God's own being. My life is not my own. It is given to me—a gift of the most personal and intimate kind.

Dust creature I may be, but I am part of something much greater. An improbable story of life, wonder and mystery stirs in me. It is renewed in me with every breath I take. So I am restless dust. I am dust that prays and hopes. I am dust with dreams of glory, of a life that is not my own and that I have barely begun to imagine.

I will remember I am a creature of the earth, but I will also attend to what I find written there in the dust of my nature. They are words of love, of life, of transformation. Dust I may be, but I am *desired* dust. Improbably, wonderfully, I am dust with a destiny.

FOR REFLECTION

Find a dusty surface and write a prayer with your finger in the dust. (If you were to return later and find that God has written a reply there, what might it be?)

CALL ME 'BITTER'

When they came to Bethlehem, the whole town was stirred because of them; and the women said, 'Is this Naomi?' She said to them, 'Call me no longer Naomi, call me Mara, for the Almighty has dealt bitterly with me. I went away full, but the Lord has brought me back empty; why call me Naomi when the Lord has dealt harshly with me, and the Almighty has brought calamity upon me?' So Naomi returned together with Ruth the Moabite, her daughter-in-law, who came back with her from the country of Moab. They came to Bethlehem at the beginning of the barley harvest.

RUTH 1:19–22

Ruth, one of the briefest books in the Bible, tells of Naomi and her family, who left Bethlehem to escape a famine. In a foreign land, her husband and two sons died in quick succession. Years later, she is returning home. She has left a land that was empty; she returns as harvest is being gathered. The emptiness is now in the heart of this widowed and weary woman.

Imagine the villagers in the fields trying to identify the distant figures on the road: 'Is it Naomi?' (her name means 'Sweet one'). It is here, in the heart of her own covenant community, that she speaks the burden of her heart. She tells her story of loss upon loss with unrestrained anger: 'Don't call me Naomi, call me "Mara" [bitter], for Shaddai has made me very bitter... Shaddai has afflicted me' (literal translation).

'Shaddai' is one of the most ancient names for the God of the Hebrew patriarchs. It is the name invoked in solemn blessing, judging and cursing, and it is used often in the book of Job. The storyteller casts Naomi's complaint in legal form, the language of someone who is coming to court to bring a complaint. Shaddai is the accused. He has not acted justly. He has been the cause of her suffering.

It is rare enough for a woman to be given a voice in the Bible, but this is a shockingly blunt language for anyone to use to God. Yet the greatest honour is paid to Naomi here. No one tries to calm her down. She is not rebuked, patronised, blamed or taken aside by a pastoral elder. Her theology is not corrected; nor is God defended or his apparent inaction excused. Her bitter complaint is recorded with utter seriousness. The community knows that her business must be with God.

We need to discover this dimension of prayer. Western churches have no tradition of protest or complaint as a valid and sometimes vital expression of faith. This is in complete contrast to the Bible, where over two-thirds of the Psalms start from cries of anger and perplexity directed at God.

I recall talking to a single mother for whom life had been constantly hard. New to churchgoing, she was struggling to cope with the relentlessly upbeat faith around her. Like Naomi, she needed to draw up her case against God and list her grievances. I found her anger unsettling, not least because, more than I cared to admit, she had a valid point. Where had God been all this time? But the hardest thing for me, as a Christian minister, was to resist trying to defend or excuse God. He needs no such protection and the Bible understands the need for this kind of praying very well. Why didn't I?

Writing about the birth of his son with a rare genetic condition, Paul Bradbury recalls his initial response—finding reasons 'why God had allowed this'. After a few days, though, some very different responses surfaced.

> *An anger ran from me towards God in a way that would have seemed blasphemous earlier in my Christian life. It burst from me in language and feelings towards God that were intense and irreverent—it was rough, raw and above all real. I had never uttered such words before in that way, with real venom and real anguish. I felt almost ashamed at this outburst. I could sense the disapproval of a church [that] finds little space for honest emotions that illuminate the negative aspects of our experience as the people of God.*[8]

Faith that can speak to God only in positive, upbeat or submissive terms is neither trusting nor reverent. It is just polite and compliant. Of what use is that in the face of God's perplexing absence or apparent inaction through the bitterest struggles of life? In the Bible, the prayer of protest is a sign of trusting faith, not of its absence.

FOR REFLECTION

Are there prayers that I have not yet found a way of expressing to God?

FIRST NAMED TERMS

There was a man of Benjamin whose name was Kish... a man of wealth. He had a son whose name was Saul, a handsome young man... head and shoulders above everyone else. Now the donkeys of Kish, Saul's father, had strayed. So Kish said to his son Saul, '... Go and look for the donkeys.' He passed through the hill country of Ephraim... the land of Shalishah... Shaalim... [and] Benjamin, but they did not find them. When they came to the land of Zuph, Saul said to the boy who was with him, 'Let us turn back, or my father will stop worrying about the donkeys and worry about us.'
1 SAMUEL 9:1–5

The storyteller of the ancient saga that the Bible calls simply '1 and 2 Samuel' used various methods of leaving clues to where the significant challenges in the unfolding drama might be found. Here is one of them. When a significant character makes a first appearance in the story, the first words they speak reveal their character, for good or ill. Samuel's first words, as a small boy in the temple, are 'Here I am!' (1 Samuel 3:4), and those words were to define his entire life. He became a great leader who was utterly present to God and to his people.

We are introduced to Saul just before he is chosen as Israel's first king. The initial signs are promising (if you are looking for such things): he is handsome, tall and imposing. We first encounter him searching for his father's lost donkeys. He does not find them, and his first words are 'Let us turn back, or my father will start worrying about us.' Sadly, this is a sign of the man and the king that he became. He was unable to finish what he began. He never found the things he was looking for. He was too easily distracted by what other people were thinking about him.

We all have our own 'first words'—the phrases or responses that express our most distinctive reactions to life. These emotional reflexes surface most clearly when we are feeling under pressure, insecure or out of our comfort zone, so they may express our fear or hesitancy: 'Help!', 'Oh no!' or 'This is too much.' Do you know what yours are? They are so much a part of us that we are often unconscious of them and need the help of those closest to us to identify them. 'First words' might also express degrees of confidence and excitement. I have a friend who is never lacking in confidence and relishes new challenges. His characteristic response is usually 'Bring it *on*'!

We could call these our 'default settings'. When we buy a computer, it comes with programmes installed. We switch it on and templates and control bars appear on the screen, ready to use. These are the default settings, installed at the factory—but we may be unaware that all these settings are negotiable. They can be changed, and they need to be changed if the machine is to become *my* equipment, doing tasks the way I need them to be done.

Our personal default settings are established very early in our lives. Authority figures such as parents and teachers are hugely influential in this process, but I agree with a therapist friend who believes that our most significant settings are learned in school playgrounds. It is there that we have our first experiences of unregulated play, learning to negotiate, handle power, take risks, manage fear and make our own choices. For all of us, some of our settings are more helpful than others.

It is important to be clear that those 'first words' in Bible stories do not fix a person's character or destiny. Rather, they highlight the aspects of a person's personality that will need to be faced if the person is to develop and mature into their full potential. It is the same for us. With each challenge and change in life, we need to revisit our default settings. The difficulty is that we can feel completely fixed: 'This is me; I cannot change who I am.' We feel trapped in a closed cycle from which we cannot seem to move on.

For Christians, the hope of change lies in the cross of Jesus. Planted in our life story, the cross cuts into those fixed cycles and makes a break in them. As our story goes around again and those familiar responses kick in, there are now moments of grace, spaces in which, however hesitantly, we can choose differently and renegotiate our default settings. Trapped cycles unravel and the threads begin to open out in unexpected, exciting directions. Our first words do not need to be our last.

PRAYER

Lord, break into my life and give me the courage to live in the adventure of all you call me to be.

MAKE IT ALL A GIFT

'You have heard that it was said, "An eye for an eye and a tooth for a tooth." But I say to you, Do not resist an evildoer. But if anyone strikes you on the right cheek, turn the other also; and if anyone wants to sue you and take your coat, give your cloak as well; and if anyone forces you to go one mile, go also the second mile. Give to everyone who begs from you, and do not refuse anyone who wants to borrow from you.'

MATTHEW 5:38–42

'An eye for an eye' (Leviticus 24:19–20) was not a legal requirement. It was a limit set by a law intended to fix a proportionate scale to retribution and stop violence escalating out of control. But in the Sermon on the Mount, Jesus goes far beyond this limit: '*I* say to you, do not resist an evildoer.' To illustrate what he means, he offers four examples.

You take a blow on the right cheek—which would be administered by the back of the right hand. In Jesus' culture there was no gesture more contemptuous or abusive, but he not only says, 'Do not resist'; he requires us to offer the other cheek too. Why respond like this? Certainly followers of Jesus should expect to be treated at times as he himself was, but that is not where Jesus puts the emphasis. This section of teaching concludes with a call to be imitators of the Father in heaven (5:45, 48). We are to reflect the likeness of God in our responses to each other.

What particular likeness are we to image? Notice that all the examples involve 'turning' and 'giving'. We are to turn the demand into a gift, to refuse to let it be an issue of power. In the life God gives, there is no place for the language of vindication, revenge, repayment and just deserts. To offer our life as a gift images heaven and imitates God.

Imagine that someone wants to sue you. What do you own? Just a coat? You are not wealthy, then. 'Give it to them,' says Jesus—'oh, and offer your cloak too.' The coat is an undergarment; the cloak is the more valuable outer garment and serves as your blanket at night. Give it all!

Being commandeered is still one of the petty humiliations of life under an occupying power, and it is as deeply resented today as it was then. 'Make it a gift,' says Jesus. 'Here, let me carry your other bag as well. Where do you live? I'll take it *all* the way—no problem.'

'Give to everyone who begs from you' is a teaching that most church treasurers would rather deny is in the Bible at all! But here is the situation reversed. This is not a response to someone oppressing me; it is about becoming an oppressor myself, by withholding what I have from those in need. Make it a gift.

There is one other important outcome when we turn everything to a gift: we refuse to be a victim. Victim mentality is very powerful in our society. We live in a culture of blame and litigation. *You* owe me. *He* forced me to. *They* made me. But when we respond like that, we are still part of the old mindset, trapped in patterns of violent competition under laws designed to try to limit the damage. Instead, take responsibility back. By the way you respond, turn a demand into a gift. Firmly, graciously insist that you are in a relationship of equals.

'I am teaching you another way,' says Jesus. Take the relationship right outside those unredeemed categories of power and rivalry. *Not* resisting is the radically new way of resisting! It does not mean being indifferent to evil and passively enduring it as part of our lot. Jesus means that we should not resist evil *on its own terms*. Do not repay evil for evil. A few verses later, he is teaching his followers to love their enemies and seek the enemies' blessing by praying for them (5:43–48). While there is any sense of wanting to win the argument, of point scoring, being proved right or wanting other people taken down, we are still trapped in the old way of thinking.

God does not meet us on those terms. God is life itself. He does not even think in terms of possession or ownership because he has no need to. Nor should we, says Jesus.

These responses are costly but they make something quite new possible. When we make a gift of it all, a trapped world is opened to the life of God and becomes a world in which even God freely gives himself.

PRAYER

Help me to turn from defending my own honour to offering my life as a gift.

WEEK 2

THE COMPASS OF OUR EXCITEMENT

IN THE BREAKING OF THE BREAD

When he was at the table with them, he took bread, blessed and broke it, and gave it to them. Then their eyes were opened, and they recognised him; and he vanished from their sight. They said to each other, 'Were not our hearts burning within us while he was talking to us on the road, while he was opening the scriptures to us?' That same hour they got up and returned to Jerusalem; and they found the eleven and their companions gathered together. They were saying, 'The Lord has risen indeed…!' Then they told what had happened on the road, and how he had been made known to them in the breaking of the bread.

LUKE 24:30–35

It is late on Easter Day. Early that morning, the tomb of Jesus was found open and empty. Strange stories are circulating, of angels and resurrection. Far from being good news, this only adds to the exhausted confusion of the disciples. Two have decided to go home. A stranger joins them on the road and they talk at length. It is Jesus but they do not recognise him. They reach their village as the light is failing and they urge him to stay with them.

The story now reaches its climax. At their meal table, the stranger becomes the host. In an action familiar in any Jewish home, he blesses the food—taking, breaking and sharing the bread. At this moment their eyes open in startled recognition: it is Jesus! This is exactly what he did at his final supper with his disciples, just days before. But while this is surely a connection that we should be making, Luke is setting the scene in a wider context.

In Luke's Gospel, meals with Jesus are occasions where significant moments of teaching and ministry happen. The issue of who he ate with was a source of great scandal. At those tables he confronted the social and religious assumptions of his day as he spoke on love, justice and the life of the coming kingdom. Prejudice and religious arrogance were exposed. There (as in many of his parables), outsiders became honoured guests (see Luke 5:27–32). Wherever Jesus was the host at a meal, a new community was called into being and God's generous welcome was declared, most vividly at the feeding of the 5000 (9:12–17). All these themes are present at the meal that Christians have celebrated ever since, in obedience to his command: 'Do this in remembrance of me' (Luke 22:19).

In no other meals in Luke's Gospel, though, are 'eyes opened'. That happens in only one other place—at the first meal in the Bible, when Adam and Eve take and eat food they have been forbidden to touch (Genesis 3:1–7). Their eyes were opened then, but not to life or joy. Catastrophic loss followed, and they were condemned to wander for ever in exile from each other, from creation and from God.

Here on the far side of death, that wandering comes to an end. The risen Jesus takes, blesses, breaks and shares the bread. Eyes are opened as before, but this time to joyful recognition. It is the eighth meal in Luke's Gospel: it is the first day of the new creation. This meal proclaims that the long exile of the human race is over. Creation is renewed. The story is beginning again.

Jesus is physically present only until he is recognised. Then he vanishes—but no one seems to notice. The resurrection stories are very sensitive to those, like us, who live and believe without physical sight of Jesus. More intimate than physical acquaintance is to know his life within. 'Did not our hearts burn within us?'

The whole story now goes into reverse. The two disciples immediately return to Jerusalem and, as they describe the event, they are very specific in recalling the moment when Jesus was recognised. He made himself known 'in the breaking of the bread'. Ever since, when Christians celebrate Communion, that moment of the breaking is very important.

Jesus is found not only where life is whole but where he willingly shares in its brokenness. There is room at this meal for lives that are fractured and *un*healed. At the time of writing, this has renewed significance for me. Perhaps it has for you, as you read. Nowhere is Jesus more needed. Nowhere do we long more to recognise him than in the wounds of lives found, for whatever reason, in far exile from 'wholeness'.

Here in this meal is the promise that Jesus is present where we need him most—as stranger or in startled recognition. Here is food to sustain all of us on the journey into the welcome and home of God's love.

PRAYER

Lord, make yourself known among those I pray for today, whose lives contain broken things, who feel lost and far from home.

LEAD US INTO TEMPTATION

Then Jesus came from Galilee to John at the Jordan, to be baptised by him... And when Jesus had been baptised, just as he came up from the water, suddenly the heavens were opened to him and he saw the Spirit of God descending like a dove and alighting on him. And a voice from heaven said, 'This is my Son, the Beloved, with whom I am well pleased.' Then Jesus was led up by the Spirit into the wilderness to be tempted by the devil. He fasted for forty days and forty nights, and afterwards he was famished. The tempter came and said to him, 'If you are the Son of God...'

MATTHEW 3:13, 16—4:3

Matthew reports this unexpected sequence of events in a very matter-of-fact way. First, we find Jesus receiving baptism, even though this is for the washing away of sin and is required only by sinners. As he emerges from the water, the heavens open. The Father names him his Son and declares his delight in him. The Spirit descends and fills him. But then, without explanation, Jesus finds himself deep in the wilderness. Matthew says that he was 'led up' there. This sounds rather bland, for in Mark's earlier account Jesus is *driven* there by the Spirit (Mark 1:12). These trials are no accident: they are arranged by God. Jesus is driven into temptation, and the devil is waiting, booked for the purpose. Even evil, it seems, must serve the purposes of God.

This is not our usual understanding of wilderness and temptation. We tend to assume that our 'desert times' are signs that our life has gone astray and perhaps that God's judgement is on us. Our temptations are symptoms of careless and undisciplined living. They are to be avoided. Trials come because we are frail and wayward. Didn't Jesus himself teach us to pray, 'Lead us not into temptation' (Matthew 6:13, NIV)?

Here at the beginning of the ministry of Jesus, we are reminded of a neglected understanding of God's presence and his work in the very same flaws and frailty of our humanity. These temptations *follow* baptism. They come to those in whom God delights and who are filled with him. This testing is a *consequence* of being filled with the Holy Spirit. These struggles are willed by God and are part of his purposes. Temptation here is a fruit of the Spirit! The challenge for us is to turn from preoccupation with our own sin and failure. Something holy and purposeful is at work in us. There is a *Christian* experience of the wilderness.

Traditional religious art depicts the descending Spirit in this scene as a delicate, pure white dove. In fact, though, the Greek word can also describe a rock dove. Neither white nor at all delicate, rock doves dwell in rugged desert terrain. The wilderness is therefore the natural habitat of the Spirit. This challenges us in the way we respond to the tests and struggles of life.

Far from erecting a benign shield around our fragilities, this wild Spirit is found deliberately driving us into life. If there are temptations to resist (and there are), there are others to give in to. This is no invitation either to selfishness or recklessness, though. Jesus' trials make that abundantly clear. The Spirit knows the difference, too, and is at work tempting us to choose life, to risk growing, to be responsible, to renounce evil and to surrender to the adventure of service in the delight of God. In his presence our complex desires, longings and choices are not tamed. They become more vivid, more vital, more focused on God. The struggle is real, and it may take us to our limits.

Jesus is here ahead of us, though. He always is. We are not called to go anywhere that he has not already been. Although there are features of his temptations that are unique to Jesus and his calling, they are not to be placed in a separate category from our own. They are a consequence and sign of his utter identification with us. He is 'in every respect… tempted as we are, yet without sin' (Hebrews 4:15), and only someone who has never given in to temptation or evil knows its full power.

In this wilderness of testing, we will certainly meet ourselves for who we truly are. This means seeing our sinfulness, but so much more. Always more important than what we turn from is who we turn to. Here we are learning security in God alone. It is to the Father's love that Jesus himself returns throughout his ministry and all his temptations.

We must learn to do the same.

PRAYER

Come, Holy Spirit, and lead me into the temptation of God.

FROM THE FAR COUNTRY

'There was a man who had two sons. The younger of them said to his father, "Father, give me the share of the property that will belong to me." So he divided his property between them. A few days later the younger son travelled to a distant country, and there he squandered his property in dissolute living. When he had spent everything, a severe famine took place throughout that country, and he began to be in need... One of the citizens of that country... sent him to his fields to feed the pigs... But when he came to himself he said, "How many of my father's hired hands have bread enough and to spare, but here I am dying of hunger! I will get up and go to my father, and I will say to him, 'Father, I have sinned against heaven and before you; I am no longer worthy to be called your son; treat me like one of your hired hands.'"'

LUKE 15:11–15, 17–19

This story is commonly called the parable of the prodigal son. Curious, that. There are two sons. Why is it named after only one, and why that one in particular? There were two groups in the audience: 'All the tax-collectors and sinners were coming near to listen to [Jesus]. And the Pharisees and the scribes were grumbling and saying, "This fellow welcomes sinners and eats with them"' (vv. 1–2).

It begins abruptly with background. The younger son goes

to his father and demands his share of the family inheritance. How the father replies, we are not told. He just accedes, giving both sons their share. No one in the audience would have needed telling that, in the society of the day, this behaviour was the gravest possible public insult to the father. Whatever the message of the story is, surely it is obvious where the finger of judgement will point at the end?

'Prodigal' means profligate, excessively wasteful, squandering. It sums up the son's life in the far country very accurately: he ends up bankrupt and friendless. His inner crisis is mirrored by the outer crisis. In the far country of his impulsive choices, everything has run out. There is famine in the land and he, a Jew, is now a swineherd, working for Gentiles. There was no greater shame.

Hebrew storytelling puts its main point in the middle, not the end—and here it is: 'He came to himself' (v. 17). This is such a revealing phrase. We speak of 'coming to our senses', which catches the same sense of a shock of recognition. Imagine enjoying a dream of wildly exciting, uninhibited adventure where (as in all dreams) no rules constrain our freedom in any way. Then we awake to discover it was real all along. We really were behaving like that! All around us, our world lies trashed and ruined—the only life that is ours to live.

The 'far country' is not just a physical place for the son. In a very significant way he has been in exile from his own self. He now sees where his behaviour and choices have led him. He knows he has blown everything. His only option is to return home and cast himself on his father's mercy. Perhaps he will be taken on as a slave, somewhere out of sight, where he will at least have food but cause no further harm.

A public figure, notorious for repeated financial problems,

is aptly described as 'driving through life with no rear-view mirror'. The way we live has consequences and they will catch us up. Someone else describes Western culture as life 'on the compass of our excitement', restlessly pursuing every quiver of the needle, driven by our appetites. The deep economic crisis of recent years was wholly predictable in an economic system driven by unsustainable assumptions of endless growth. But has anything changed? Consumer debt has tripled in the last 20 years. Meanwhile, my bank presently offers me higher interest rates for my current account than for my savings accounts—on the condition that I *spend*. It is a wasteful dream in every way. Recent surveys in the UK reveal a society that is throwing away ten billion pounds' worth of edible food every year. We are prodigal but not yet at the point, through despair or wisdom, of coming to ourselves. A feature of people struggling with compulsive and addictive behaviour is that they cannot be helped until they hit rock bottom. You have to be desperate enough.

There may be something to envy in this young man's moment of truthful awakening—and, for one half of Jesus' audience, this story is laying bare their deepest need.

PRAYER

Lord, whatever journey I am on, bring me to myself.

THE UNLIVED LIFE

*'Now his elder son was in the field and… heard music and dancing…
He called one of the slaves and asked what was going on. He replied,
"Your brother has come, and your father has killed the fatted calf,
because he has got him back safe and sound." Then he became angry
and refused to go in. His father came out and began to plead with
him. But he answered his father, "Listen! For all these years I have
been working like a slave for you, and I have never disobeyed your
command; yet you have never given me even a young goat so that I
might celebrate with my friends. But… you killed the fatted calf for
him!" Then the father said, "Son, you are always with me, and all
that is mine is yours. But we had to celebrate and rejoice, because
this brother of yours was dead and has come to life; was lost and has
been found."'*

LUKE 15:25–32

'If you hadn't ended up doing "x", what would you have
done instead?' This is always a lively conversation-starter
over drinks or a meal. And we always know: we can all tell
'what if' or 'if only' stories of the lives we might have lived,
had things turned differently. Whether as playful fantasy or
matters of serious regret, 'our unlived lives—the wished-for
lives—are often more important to us than our so-called
lived lives,' writes Adam Phillips.[9]

It would be so interesting to know how the older son would have answered that question. He appears to have been a model son and heir, responsible and dutiful. Where was he when his profligate brother limped home penniless? He was outside *working*, of course.

As Jesus began to tell this story, it was sinners who were coming near to listen. Now, in the story, the 'good' son is coming near but, at the sound of the celebrations, he stays outside. As his father tries to persuade him to join the party, all restraint gives way. From beneath the surface of a faithful son, a festering well of bitterness overflows. He disowns his brother ('this son of yours') and accuses his father of slavery, neglect and favouritism. Here is a personality eaten away because of an unlived life—resentful, judging, envious, angry, ungrateful, unforgiving and loveless. While the younger son wasted his inheritance by living too wildly, the older wasted his by never living at all. He too was prodigal.

'You never gave me anything,' he grumbles. 'It was all yours all along,' is the father's reply. It was all there to be entered and lived. Remember, both sons received their share of the inheritance. The older one too had choices, but his share went unused and uncelebrated. So in the end, who was furthest from the father's home and love? One son needed to return to his true home from the far country of his own indulgence and impulsiveness. The other must find a way home from the bitter fruits of his own 'goodness'.

Where does this find you? The shock of the story—especially to the devoutly religious in the audience—is that the son who takes such wildly irresponsible risks with his desires is received home with unconditional joy. The brother who has been 'good', never partied or risked his dreams, never celebrated the free gift of his inheritance, is standing outside in the misery of self-chosen exile.

There is a saying that there is room for only one rebel in a family, but there are perils in self-conscious goodness and conformity, too. Repeated social surveys reveal attitudes of blame and little sympathy among the more well-off public for those who fall into debt or whose choices or misfortunes have left them needing help to rebuild their lives. Religious practice can result in the same hardening of heart. Goodness is not grace. When this story is discussed in church groups, the sympathy is often with the older son. The younger son did wrong, but he got the party. It is not fair. Sacrificial, hardworking, faithful people can be very resentful when the attention and excitement is focused on outsiders: 'You never made a fuss of me like that.'

In an imagined conversation, author Michael Gallagher asks Jesus, 'When you look at us, at me, what grieves you most?' Jesus replies, 'The unlived life. The prison of small-ness. And more terrible evils that spring from the shrinking of the heart.'[10]

There was a mission in a town, throughout which the faithful congregation struggled with the outward focus of it all. On the final evening there was an invitation to any to come forward as a mark of new commitment to Christ. There was a pause and then, to the surprise of all, one of the most respected, lifelong church members walked rapidly up the aisle, nervous and tearful. She told of a homecoming. 'I have been running for 20 years,' she said.

PRAYER

Lord, I wish to live all that is yet unlived in me.

THE PRODIGAL FATHER

[To the younger son] 'While he was still far off, his father saw him and was filled with compassion; he ran and put his arms around him and kissed him. Then the son said to him, "Father, I have sinned against heaven and before you; I am no longer worthy to be called your son." But the father said to his slaves, "Quickly, bring out a robe—the best one—and put it on him; put a ring on his finger and sandals on his feet. And get the fatted calf and kill it, and let us eat and celebrate; for this son of mine was dead and is alive again; he was lost and is found!" And they began to celebrate.'

[To the older son] '"Son, you are always with me, and all that is mine is yours. But we had to celebrate and rejoice, because this brother of yours was dead and has come to life; he was lost and has been found."'

LUKE 15:22–23, 31–32

Linked for ever to the younger son in this parable, the word 'prodigal' is assumed to mean something negative, similar to words such as wasteful, profligate and self-indulgent. But it has a positive meaning too. It describes behaviour that is overwhelmingly generous, over the top—a giving without restrain. A prodigious feat, similarly, is one that is greatly beyond the normal level.

Meet the father in this story. Though publicly humiliated

and abandoned by his younger son, the father has never stopped waiting and hoping. Imagine him, day after day, eyes scanning the horizon from a seat by the window. The father is a prodigal too—prodigal in love, longing and mercy. If we miss this meaning of the word, we miss what makes this story so shocking and so hopeful.

One day, as his vigil is resumed, a stooped, ragged figure appears in the distance at the end of the trail. The father strains forward. Surely not! Then without hesitation he gathers up his robes and goes running to meet his son. Old men do not run in that culture. One writer with long experience of Middle Eastern society even suggests that one reason why the father runs is in order to intercept his son before the villagers reach him and lynch him, so great is the shame he has inflicted on the community.[11]

The son begins his speech but is ignored. He is swept away on hugs, kisses and preparations for the celebration. No welcome could be expressed more unconditionally.

This story is a typical example of the utter disproportion that runs through the teaching of Jesus when he speaks of divine love. All that rejoicing in heaven over just one who repents. All that trouble to find and celebrate one lost sheep while the rest of the flock are left on their own on the hillside. All those people beyond any measure of social or religious acceptability who find themselves in the honoured seats at the sumptuous banquet of the king.

The father, insulted in different ways by both his sons, reaches out to each of them, and he is wholly ungrudging as he does so. There is no blame. He has no interest in preserving his own honour or public reputation. His response bypasses every expected measure of justice, punishment, deserving or reward. This father's love endures beyond all rejection—and, of course, the presence of Jesus takes the story to another level. Divine love comes searching for the lost. This is memorably expressed in a prayer at the end of the Communion service where God the Father is thanked that 'when we were still far off you met us in your Son and brought us home'.[12]

Here we have it. Our most hesitant movement towards God draws from him a response out of all proportion. He comes running. The mark of his love is extravagant welcome, and this, says Jesus to his divided audience, is how God loves you.

A prodigal father is at the centre of this story. It is he who lives out the greatest profligacy. When we come to ourselves, it will be to discover that a wild, unconditional, prodigal love is the source of all our living. 'We love because he first loved us' (1 John 4:19). We desire because God desired us first.

So what of our own inheritance? What does such love say to us as we reflect on the mixture of freedom or constraint with which we are living out our lives? When the Father speaks to us, do we need to hear him say 'Come home' or 'You never asked'?

FOR REFLECTION AND PRAYER

Which prayer do I need to pray today: 'Father, I want to come home to your love' or 'Father, I want to risk the adventure of the life you have given me'?

THE PLAYGROUND FOR PRAYER

[Her] Let him kiss me with the kisses of his mouth!
For your love is better than wine,
your anointing oils are fragrant,
your name is perfume poured out…
Draw me after you, let us make haste.

[He] O fairest among women…
Ah, you are beautiful, my love;
ah, you are beautiful;
your eyes are doves.
SONG OF SONGS 1:2–4, 8, 15

Without any preliminaries, this poem opens with a cry of uninhibited desire. Nor should English translations deflect from the erotic immediacy of it. The text actually says, 'Your love*making* is better than wine.'

This is a strange poem to find in the Bible. It contains no direct references to God, prayer or any religious activity. The relationship it celebrates is outside marriage. Yet it is found in the holy scriptures of a conservative, patriarchal society, and throughout history only two other books of the Bible have had more commentaries written on them.

Some instinct tells us that this song is central to all we seek—and so it is, for it celebrates everything that humanity most yearns for. Here is creation restored from its ancient threefold rupture—the separation of humans from each other (expressed in the severed union of woman and man), the separation between humans and the natural world, and the separation of humans from God.

The song is a celebration of homecoming from exile to the original garden of God's good creating. The woman and man embrace in unashamed, playful delight and ecstatic mutuality. Around them, everything in the garden is in full bloom, and the assault on the senses is overpowering. Fruit is ripe; birds are singing; 'the winter is passed' (2:11). Creation is complete in itself and at one with the delight of the lovers. Woven subtly through all this, and no less erotic, are poetic allusions to and metaphors of the temple and the Torah. In a way that Christians through history have consistently struggled to do, this poem celebrates an utterly positive view of sexual desire as mutual gift in the goodness of creation. Eros here is a partner in the expression of worship, prayer and devotion. It is not to be separated off without impoverishing the whole. Indeed, there is, in eros, an energy that prayer and holiness need.

We need to hear this. The word 'sexuality' is too commonly assumed to refer to the physical expression of our desires. This narrow definition reflects the preoccupations of a highly sexualised agenda and, perhaps, an anxious church. The word certainly includes our desire for and sharing of physical pleasure but it is far more than this. It encompasses the deepest gift and mystery of our humanity as men and women. Our sexuality involves the whole of our being—

body, mind, soul and relationships—not one limited expression of it. Sexuality and spirituality are therefore intimately linked. In Song of Songs, human sexuality is an expression of our life in God, so what we call our 'spiritual' life needs living in, around and within a positive awareness of our sexuality. Angela Tilby memorably describes our sexuality as 'the playground for prayer. It is where we tumble over our greatest needs and hungers.'[13] In other words, it is where our truest humanity is explored and expressed.

The journey towards intimacy of any kind is a uniquely vulnerable one. It can be painful, slow and elusive: 'I sought him, but found him not '(3:1, 2). The song knows well the anguish, loss and wounds of love. When our search to give and receive in loving intimacy is happening in a culture where familiar guides and supports for human belonging have all but collapsed, it can become, for many, an experience of wounding, grief and shame. We need to trust that when those wounds go too deep and the most hesitant touch of a hand is all we dare offer, 'just as much love is made'.[14]

What is so positively affirmed here is that our faithful expressions of intimacy, tentative and incomplete in themselves, are a participation in what the song celebrates so vividly—life joyfully, passionately restored and awakened in the fullness of God's creating delight.

'We are destined to be makers of love, whether genitally or more diffused,' wrote Jim Cotter. 'God has created you a sexual being. God is at the heart of your striving, still creating you, always pursuing, luring, drawing, never letting go. Whatever your unique mix and measure of sexuality, be very glad: to be a human sexual is fundamental and ordinary and exceptional.'[15]

PRAYER

Lord, whether I am joyful or fearful, whole or wounded,
thank you for being at the heart and healing of my most
intimate loving.

BEING PRESENT

O Lord, you have searched me and known me.
You know when I sit down and when I rise up;
you discern my thoughts from far away...
You hem me in, behind and before...
Such knowledge is too wonderful for me...
Where can I go from your spirit?
Or where can I flee from your presence?...
Search me, O God, and know my heart...
and lead me in the way everlasting.

PSALM 139:1–2, 5–7, 23–24

I have a childhood memory of visiting a house that had a plaque on the dining room wall, over the piano. It read:

Christ is the Head of this house
The Unseen Guest at every meal
The Silent Listener to every conversation.

I am sure it was an expression of sincere faith in that home but I confess it made me anxious. I heard it as a warning: God was monitoring my every word and thought, and I was sure he would not like what he saw of me. With the best of intentions, there are ways of speaking of God's presence and knowledge that feel oppressive. They awaken the anxiety that God is surely judging rather than enjoying us. I used to play for a Christian football team that prayed together in the centre circle before the game started. I never said so but I felt robbed of the unselfconscious pleasure of just playing football. I could never quite believe that God was being invited to be other than the divine referee: add to that plaque, 'The Judge of all bad language and foul play'!

This psalm is a challenge to me. God's knowledge of all is a source of delight and security for the psalmist. He doesn't find it oppressive. He does not feel spied on. It amazes and overwhelms him by turns. The word 'wonderful' keeps recurring. Furthermore, he is utterly grateful that he cannot escape God's presence. As the psalm closes, his response is a trusting prayer that he would be even more known by God, to the very depths of his heart.

When we speak of God being near or far away, or of 'seeking God's presence', what do we actually mean? There are certainly times when we may be particularly aware of his presence and times when he seems absent. But in God 'we live and move and have our being,' says Paul (Acts 17:28), so how can such a God be distant? Augustine agrees: 'God is closer to me than I am to myself.' The problem, he laments to God, is that 'you were ever within and I was outside myself'.[16] Etty Hillesum says the same thing a different way: 'There is a really deep well inside me, and in it dwells God. Sometimes I am there too.'[17]

This means that the familiar problem with our praying or spiritual life does not lie in finding the place where God is. The idea that we are separated from God is an illusion. The problem we face is being present to *ourselves*. We can and do live at some distance from ourselves.

A practice of meditation called 'mindfulness' has been growing in popularity in recent years. This simple method is a rediscovery of an insight known in all ancient spiritual traditions and is found to be remarkably effective in helping people to manage stress, depression and anxiety. In the UK it is being taught as a part of mental health care, as well as in the high-pressure worlds of media, politics and business.

Mindfulness is a way of practising being present to ourselves and, therefore, to life itself. Once we do so, it becomes apparent how distant we have grown. As Robert MacFarlane writes, 'We experience, as no historical period before, disembodiment. We have in many ways forgotten what the world feels like. We have come increasingly to forget that our minds are shaped by the bodily experience of being in the world.'[18]

Quite simply, the starting place is our own body. Sit in an upright chair with both feet on the ground. Then quietly become aware of your physical body. Notice your breathing as it flows in and out of the body. Just that. 'The only way to explain is to suggest you try,' writes one practitioner. 'Right now. Close your eyes and bring your attention into your body, the movements of your breath, the expansion of your rib cage. Patiently. Try it for two minutes.'

FOR REFLECTION

Do as suggested above, practising 'mindfulness' for two minutes.

IN THE MIDST OF LIFE

GLORIOUS SCARS

When it was evening on that day, the first day of the week, and the doors of the house where the disciples had met were locked for fear of the Jews, Jesus came and stood among them and said, 'Peace be with you.' After he said this, he showed them his hands and his side. Then the disciples rejoiced when they saw the Lord. Jesus said to them again, 'Peace be with you. As the Father has sent me; so I send you.' When he had said this, he breathed on them and said to them, 'Receive the Holy Spirit.'

JOHN 20:19–22

Those wounds. Who would have expected to find them on the body of the person who just been raised in triumph over sin and death? The risen body of Jesus, in the fullness of new life, is still wounded. They change everything, those wounds. It is through them that the traumatised disciples recognise him with joy.

On his hands and his side, the wounds correspond to those that Jesus received on the cross. So the person who now stands before them alive is the one who was crucified. Whatever we mean by the victory of Christ, it does not leave the cross behind.

When these stories at the end of the Gospels are followed in their chronological sequence, there is a tendency to understand them as 'before-and-after' events in which one finishes and then the next starts. So the crucifixion begins and ends; then risen life starts; then Pentecost arrives. But in this passage John weaves together Good Friday, Easter Day and Pentecost into one whole event. The risen one is the crucified one who now sends out his followers with his Spirit. The commission could not be more personal. They receive his own breath ('He breathed on them'). This is a reminder of that moment in the original creation when God breathed into the nostrils of a human figure shaped from the earth and he 'became a living being' (Genesis 2:7). Creation is beginning again and, as it does so, risen life leads us towards Good Friday and Pentecost simultaneously. The risen Jesus has not ceased to be crucified. The one who is crucified and risen gives the Spirit and sends us out. So life in the Spirit is the way of the crucified, lived through his risen life.

There has been a tendency in the indexes of church hymn books to separate Good Friday and Easter. When that happens, suffering/death and victory/risen life are easily separated too. Charles Wesley is almost the only hymn writer to celebrate the significance of the scene in our reading today (in his hymn 'Lo, he comes with clouds descending'). For him, as for the first disciples, it is a source of joy and wonder.

Those dear tokens of his passion
still his dazzling body bears…
With what rapture
gaze we on those glorious scars.

Like many, I have longed for but struggled with the risen life. It is elusive and my failure can easily leave me feeling daunted and condemned. It was a relief when I discovered that I was not alone. I am deeply drawn to the suffering and crucified Jesus. I love him for his passionate, costly identification with me in my humanity. But once he is on the other side of Easter, in his risen presence, gloriously whole, he would surely have to leave me behind—for, if Easter is life raised, whole and perfect, then what place can we have in such risen life?

If there are no marks on the risen Jesus, then resurrection is only for the unmarked. But when we see him, his hands open towards us, scarred, we may dare to celebrate that we are risen too. This is *our* humanity that we see before us. In his wounds we recognise our own. Christ is one with us, sharing and bearing our story into new life.

On Easter night, during the vigil of resurrection, there is an ancient symbolic ritual. Into a large Paschal candle five spikes are pressed, representing the wounds of Jesus on the cross. Then these words are spoken: 'By his holy and glorious wounds, may Christ our Lord guard us and keep us.'

PRAYER

Come to us, risen Lord. Find us where we are locked in with our fears, elaborately guarded with bolts, chains and secure defences. They are surely no problem to you. Seek us with the story we have heard but are still unable to understand or trust.

C.S. Lewis once suggested that you can pass through our walls because you are more solid, more real, not less. So stand in our midst. Show us your wounds. May resurrection be found here where life most contradicts or resists it. Let this rising begin from the very places of defeat and despair where faith keeps slipping from our grasp. Risen Jesus, thank you for your wounds.

SNAKES AND DOVES

'See, I am sending you out like sheep into the midst of wolves; so be wise as serpents and innocent as doves.'
MATTHEW 10:16

When we list the qualities we expect to find in a follower of Jesus, 'being snake-like' is not usually one of them—but here it is, in a neglected part of the text. Older versions of the Church of England ordination service included a quaint petition that the candidate would 'be ordained with all innocency of virtue in the midst of this naughty world', but there was no prayer that they would learn snake-like behaviour. And why not? Jesus here calls us to both qualities.

I once discussed these verses with a study group and began by asking them what serpent qualities they thought Jesus wanted to see in his followers. Ideas came thick and fast and with a lot of laughter: 'wily, cunning, close to the ground, agile, knowing when to strike, watchful, lethal, dangerous…' The trouble is that they don't all sound very godly. How would you expect to recognise a *Christian* snake?

Listing the dove-like qualities proved much harder and, to be honest, a whole lot less fun: 'pure, untainted, guileless, good, harmless…' It all sounded worthy but dull. The group seemed to lose all its energy. Now, there is an innocence that makes for wonderful comedy when characters like Mr Bean are wandering around oblivious to the chaos they are leaving in their wake, but to live unaware in this world is simply dangerous. Pursued as a way of faith, it is both lifeless and godless.

Perhaps a problem is the tendency to think of innocence as a kind pre-experience, as in the 'innocence of childhood'. It is a kind of moral virginity. Once lost or surrendered, it cannot be restored. But such innocence is not only untainted by corruption, it is untouched by any goodness either. There is no life on offer at all.

If Jesus calls us to innocence, it is not something we are born with. Innocence is something we must learn, and learning to be a dove also requires learning to be like a snake. Christian character is forged in the midst of costly and hazardous engagement with life, not by keeping a safe, self-protecting distance from it. Jesus was teaching the same when he called his followers to be salt in the world (Matthew 5:13). If salt is to do its work of flavouring, preserving or disinfecting, it must absorb and be absorbed.

'Wise' is the word that traditionally describes the Eastern travellers who brought gifts to the baby Jesus, but it is also used of the snake in the garden of Eden (Genesis 3:1).[19] This is alarming if we assume that snake to be the embodiment of evil and everything we should avoid. In fact, though, the creation story asserts no such thing. The snake is a creature of noteworthy cunning/wisdom, but a creature nevertheless. Jesus calls us to a thoroughly earthy, streetwise involvement in life that does not itself become corrupting, and an innocence that is not 'pure' separation. What is striking about the stories of Jesus is that many of those who presumed their own purity were revealed as snakes, while those who had been forced to the edge and assumed to be feral, beyond faith and God, often heard and received the message of Jesus with joy. In the Gospel, snakes and doves are not always what they first seem, which is perhaps another way of saying that not all snakes are poisonous.

Christian faith is for living with open eyes. We are to be nobody's fool. We recognise the tactics and the power games that control so much of life—after all, we are snakes—but we renounce them for ourselves. So where does all this leave us? Snakes that need to become more dove-like? Doves who must risk coming down to earth more? Of course, we are never wholly one or the other.

In these contradictory images Jesus is reversing our familiar assumptions of power and vulnerability. There is a willed vulnerability here that, by any other worldly measure, is plain madness. But this is about the redeeming of all those strategies for life, power and transformation. As followers of Jesus, as sheep among wolves, we are to live in this world with innocent cunning and cunning innocence.

We are not abandoned in the wilderness of this world. Jesus is the good shepherd. We are here at his bidding. We can trust him. But there is no safe living on offer. Christian faith is for living in the wild.

PRAYER

Lord, teach me to walk through this world with innocent wisdom that remains innocent—an innocence that is wise.

LIVING IN PEACE

'Peace I leave with you; my peace I give to you. I do not give to you as the world gives. Do not let your hearts be troubled, and do not let them be afraid.'

JOHN 14:27

When I try to imagine what the peace of God is like, I tend to start from my best experiences of earthly peace. Surely it is like those—only deeper, more wonderful and longer lasting? But that is precisely what Jesus says it is *not*. He says, 'It is *not* as the world gives.'

That much should be obvious from any reading of the stories about Jesus. His actions and words often provoked furious conflict and division. He himself said, 'I have not come to bring peace, but a sword' (Matthew 10:34). For one called 'Prince of Peace', he did a lot of peace breaking! In fact, it seems that the peace of Jesus can only be received once the peace of this world has been exposed as false and shattered.

If so, then the way we speak of Christian peace needs much more care. I often pass a church that has posters on its noticeboard. At the time of writing, the picture is of sunlit, snow-capped mountains mirrored perfectly in the tranquil surface of the lake in the valley below. The caption is 'Be still and know that I am God'. People are totally absent from this scene. So is anything we might call 'ordinary life'. The peace in this picture is an absence. It is an escape. When I say to someone, 'Just leave me in peace', I am using this definition of the word. I want something to go away. This kind of peace can only happen when things that 'disturb my peace' are missing—stress, problems and so on. Linking the biblical text to this scene suggests that Christian peace offers precisely that kind of escape. But if peace is available only where certain conditions are met—where there is no conflict, only the beautiful parts of creation are acknowledged, and normal life is absent—then only a privileged few can ever enjoy it. It is certainly not on offer in daily living.

The peace of Jesus is not the absence of something but the presence of someone. It is a gift in the midst of life at its most burdened and stressful, not an escape from it. That is why it is good news for hearts that are troubled. The word *shalom* in the Bible, which we often translate as 'peace', does not focus on feelings at all (though these may be present). In fact, *shalom* is concerned with harmony at all levels of life, including international relations and within societies and communities. Its goal is the reconciliation of humanity and all creation in God, and the establishing of Christ's rule of justice and mercy.

Peace that is 'not as the world gives' may not be easy to recognise. It may feel contradictory. The peace of Jesus disturbed comfortable people when he confronted ways of living that were based on privilege, exclusion or avoidance. Praying for peace is not about seeking a quiet life. It may actually be the peace of Jesus that is doing the disturbing. For the peace of Jesus to reach me, he must break through all my self-created securities and refuges. They must all go.

The peace of Jesus is also comfort to the disturbed. Stories of encounters between Jesus and disturbed people are among the most moving in the Gospels, and such encounters still are today. There is a prayer that speaks of God's peace as 'passing all understanding'. That is good news. To be held secure in God's peace does not require our understanding, which is often beyond us anyway. When the writer and speaker Henri Nouwen suffered an emotional breakdown, there were times when his friends would lie beside him and just hold him tightly. For much of that time, he was beyond conversation and too traumatised even to be aware of them. In biblical terms, he was held in their *shalom*, beyond understanding, on the journey into healing.

Many Christian communities conclude their worship with the words 'Go in peace', but if we think it means 'Go home feeling peaceful', we have missed the point. The invitation is to something so much bigger, more wonderful and altogether more challenging. I remember someone coming to me after a service and saying, 'When I heard the words "Go in peace" I felt I was being invited to enter somewhere.' That is exactly what they mean. Go *into shalom*; go into the place where God reigns; may you enter where his love and justice is known; may his peace keep you on the journey; go from here and be part of the means by which his kingdom of peace will come on earth.'

PRAYER

Lord, lead me into your shalom.

WEDNESDAY

TAKING SIDES

There were some present who told him about the Galileans whose blood Pilate had mingled with their sacrifices. He asked them, 'Do you think that because these Galileans suffered in this way they were worse sinners than all other Galileans? No, I tell you; but unless you repent, you will all perish as they did. Or those eighteen who were killed when the tower of Siloam fell on them—do you think that they were worse offenders than all the others living in Jerusalem? No, I tell you; but unless you repent, you will all perish just as they did.'
LUKE 13:1–5

This is an unexpected response to a story of an atrocity. Jesus is expected to take sides here, and he will surely find against Pilate and vindicate the innocent victims. Isn't it clear who is good and who is bad? But Jesus expresses no pity. He offers no comment on Pilate, the victims or God. He refuses to takes sides at all. Instead he issues a blunt call to repentance. A world like ours, that gives high priority to 'rights' and the apportioning of blame, will find this teaching offensive.

He then reminds his disciples of another locally known disaster that involved no immediate human agency, good or bad. A tower had collapsed, killing 18 people. Jesus' response is the same. He seems unmoved by the actual events, the fate of the victims or any question of where God was in it all.

Instead he repeats the same warning: 'Unless you repent, you will all perish just as they did.'

Elsewhere in the Gospels, religious buildings meet the same indifference as human oppression and natural disaster. When a disciple expresses awe at the sheer magnificence of the holy temple, Jesus replies, 'Not one stone will be left here upon another; all will be thrown down' (Mark 13:1–2).

How would we react if Jesus spoke to us like that? Imagine him sitting with us today as we press him to respond to the issues that concern us most. We tell him stories of a natural disaster in the news. We tell of the treatment of asylum seekers, victims of war or poverty, child abuse and violence against women or the LGBT community. Perhaps we share with him our vision for Christian faith in our land. But he doesn't seem interested at all. He doesn't treat these events as offering any 'sign of the times' or carrying divine meaning. He doesn't speak against Islamism, debt or consumerism, or advocate equality or sexual inclusion. He attaches no special value to the church as an institution. He refuses to involve God in the discussion at all. But the warning is the same: 'Unless you repent, you will all perish.' 'Repent' simply means 'turn' or 'change direction'. We must turn—surrendering again and again all our attempts at understanding this simply from our own viewpoint.

James Alison is a theological teacher who has known victimisation and exclusion because he is gay. He therefore reads these words from among those in society who have more reason and need than most to hear the advocacy of Jesus for their cause. 'What exactly must we repent of?' he asks.[20]

First, we must repent of our assumptions that God's action is tied to our agendas or the hopes of any one group or campaign issue. Jesus is not a partisan. Beware of presuming whose side he is on or that God's response is in any way determined by our own sense of what is important. This is hard to hear when our stories contain genuine pain and injustice, but, for Jesus, the 'good' and 'innocent' here are in just as much peril as the 'bad'. Both are called to repentance.

Second, we need to repent of the ways we seek 'meaning' in the events of the world. Out of self-interest or insecurity, the temptation is to establish our place and significance in the world by claiming that our own desires, preferences and enthusiasms have a special significance to God. Once we start giving sacred meaning to our longings and struggles, we end up trapped in a world of rivalry, exclusion and reciprocal violence—and we assume that God is too. We should remember that, after his comments on the temple, Jesus warned about misinterpreting signs and following false messiahs (Mark 13:5–23).

Yet we must still search for meaning and purpose in the events of life, and we cannot but seek God in all of this. The warning here is about where we look and the conclusions we are tempted to draw.

Jesus is not indifferent, of course. It's just that the story he is telling is so much bigger.

PRAYER

Lord, I repent of all my attempts to use you for my own ends and needs. I turn towards the bigger story of your love.

BEING HUMAN

'"Lord, when was it that we saw you hungry and gave you food, or thirsty and gave you something to drink? And when was it that we saw you a stranger and welcomed you, or naked and gave you clothing? And when was it that we saw you sick or in prison and visited you?" And the king will answer them, "Truly I tell you, just as you did it to one of the least of these... you did it to me."'
MATTHEW 25:37–40

Jesus tells the story of a man travelling from Jerusalem to Jericho (Luke 10:25–37). On the way he is attacked, robbed, stripped of everything and left close to death. As he is naked, there is no way of identifying him from his clothing. He is unconscious, so there is no way to locate him by his accent or language. He is at the point of death, so there is no way to check if he is still alive without risking the ritual defilement that follows touching a dead body. So there he lies, beyond any discernible racial, religious, social or medical categories— and that is precisely the point. He is simply a human being in need.

As he lies there, two religious officials pass by without helping, even crossing the road to avoid him. The next traveller stops and helps, at considerable risk to himself. Not only is he in bandit country; he is a Samaritan, travelling though a region where Samaritans are hated. This is not a place to linger, but he does just that and more.

As part of a psychology experiment, a group of trainee ministers were once asked to prepare presentations on 'the modern meaning of the parable of the good Samaritan'. They were told when they would present their work, but then they were interrupted and told that the event had been unavoidably brought forward. They were to proceed urgently to the lecture room. In the passageway leading to the venue, a man lay on the floor, groaning. The students' reactions to him were observed. Only ten per cent stopped to offer help; a number actually stepped over the body to get to the hall. The research found that the more rushed we are, and the more self-aware we feel about our significance in the demands of life or faith, the more dehumanised our responses tend to become. And religion can be as preoccupying as anything else in life, possibly more so.[21]

One of the core obligations in the Bible is to welcome the stranger—because God does it. But this welcome is much more than a greeting or meal. It is a commitment to the needs of a whole society. God 'executes justice for the orphan and the widow, and... loves the strangers, providing them with food and clothing. You shall also love the stranger, for you were strangers in the land of Egypt' (Deuteronomy 10:18–19). Nor is this welcome offered on any preferential terms, such as race, gender, social class, religion, wealth or influence. A 'stranger' cannot yet be categorised in any of these ways. Jesus takes this teaching further: 'Just as you did it to one of the least of these... you did it to me' (Matthew 25:40). God does not just care for the stranger and call us to do the same. The stranger is where we meet him. The face of the stranger is his face, so to reject the stranger is to reject him. To exclude the widow is to exclude God.

St Benedict taught, 'Let all guests be received like Christ, for he is going to say, "I came as a guest, and you received me." And to all let honour be shown, let all humility be shown. Let the whole body be prostrated on the ground in adoration of Christ, who indeed is received in their persons.'[22] With practical directness, Benedict's followers would weave this message into their daily tasks. When a wayfarer arrived at a monastery asking for food, the message would go to the kitchens, 'Jesus is at the door'.

How might this challenge the way we look at others and welcome them? It has been described as living with an 'unboundaried heart'.[23] Such a welcome is not for effect or for achieving anything. It is an unmeasured, unbounded gift.

Did you notice the reaction of the people in today's passage, when they are commended for their care? They are completely baffled: 'When did we care for *you*, Lord?' (vv. 38–39). They did not recognise the king. Their welcome and care for those in need were not offered out of self-conscious service to a religious creed or ideology. Perhaps they were not even trying to be good. They were just being human—like God.

PRAYER

Jesus, help me to see you in those I meet today.

EVERY BUSH IS BURNING

Moses was keeping the flock of his father-in-law Jethro, the priest of Midian; he led his flock beyond the wilderness, and came to Horeb, the mountain of God. There the angel of the Lord appeared to him in a flame of fire out of a bush; he looked, and the bush was blazing, yet it was not consumed. Then Moses said, 'I must turn aside and look at this great sight, and see why the bush is not burned up.' When the Lord saw that he had turned aside to see, God called to him out of the bush, 'Moses, Moses!' And he said, 'Here I am.' Then he said, 'Come no closer! Remove the sandals from your feet, for the place on which you are standing is holy ground.'

EXODUS 3:1–5

Imagine a day like any other—the sun already oppressively hot, the landscape unforgivingly parched and stony. A shepherd is leading his flock on the daily search for water and grazing. Out of the corner of his eye he sees a bush burning. In that heat it is not unusual for a shrub simply to catch fire and be reduced to ashes in seconds, but this bush goes on burning. The shepherd turns aside, wanders over—and finds himself face to face with God.

So begins the famous story of the journey of God's people out of slavery in Egypt and the revelation of their God as saviour and liberator. This story of deliverance has been an inspiration for oppressed peoples and communities around the world ever since.

Now, in the world in which I grew up, curiosity was frowned upon. It was rude to stare or point: 'Don't be nosey.' The proverbial wisdom warned that 'curiosity killed the cat', but the story of the exodus cannot begin without it. It must all depend on a bored shepherd in the wilderness being inquisitive enough to break his routine and take a closer look at something unusual. How many burning bushes he had missed before this one, we do not know. Knowing how hard it can be for others to get my attention at times, I can easily imagine a trail of smoking ash piles tracking back behind Moses across the wilderness.

Jesus often taught that the things that matter in life are not on the surface or planted on the path in front of us. They are hidden. We need eyes open, senses alert. God is never so clearly revealed as to be obvious. 'What's that over there, sticking out of the grass? Perhaps it's been left exposed by the recent rain. Could be nothing, but let's have a look…' And from such chance, inquisitive beginnings, a person finds a priceless treasure trove buried in the field. In the other parable of Jesus, the finding is not a matter of chance. The treasure is hidden somewhere in the depths of the sea. So in one story we must go digging; in the other we must go diving. In both we must go searching.

The story of Moses illustrates the importance of 'peripheral vision'. Peripheral vision allows you to see what you are *not* looking at. It is on the edge of the main focus of our sight: we are looking out of the corner of our eye. Like Moses, when we become aware of it, we think of it as a distraction. The medical condition in which peripheral sight is missing is called 'tunnel vision'. The term has become a metaphor for the most narrow and inflexible approaches to life, and religious life can be especially vulnerable to it.

Gandalf the wizard, in J.R.R. Tolkien's 'Lord of the Rings' trilogy, offers an important role model here. He takes peripheral vision very seriously, always wandering off, turning aside and paying close attention to things that other people find of little interest or value—hobbits, for example. His impatient peers mock him for his eccentricities, but time and again, when the need is great, he can draw from an unexpected source of wisdom that eludes others altogether.

Real faith is inquisitive and adventurous. The challenge is to let life inconvenience us. We must be willing to break our routines and go wandering. We must risk arriving late, or not at all! Such faith is never so focused that it misses what is waiting out there on the periphery of our vision.

So I will sit for a moment. I will let my vision range. Who knows what might be waiting for me to notice? Like Moses and his people, we are part of something so much bigger. There is always another story, waiting to break the surface. Perhaps every bush is burning.

PRAYER

Lord, distract me—so that I may catch sight of you in unexpected places.

THE WILES OF THE DEVIL

Finally, be strong in the Lord and in the strength of his power. Put on the whole armour of God, so that you may be able to stand against the wiles of the devil. For our struggle is not against enemies of blood and flesh, but against the rulers, against the authorities, against the cosmic powers of this present darkness, against the spiritual forces of evil in the heavenly places. Therefore take up the whole armour of God, so that you may be able to withstand on that evil day, and having done everything, to stand firm.

EPHESIANS 6:10–13

Along with many Christians around the world today, Paul knew all too well that he was in a costly battle for his faith. He wrote those words from prison and, perhaps with few other distractions on offer, he used the armour and weapons of the Roman guard next to him to meditate on discipleship as active combat.

'Be strong in the Lord.' The first priority is to have a right confidence in God and his power, but there are tough realities to be faced in this world. One of them is the presence of evil. There has been much debate about what Paul is actually teaching here. He rather assumes that his readers will understand. For Paul, evil powers are active in the world, resisting its transformation in the love of God. Their final defeat is assured but, until that day, we must stand firm and know the weapons of our faith.

There are two dangers, one of which is to see evil everywhere and seek no other explanation. Some religious groups fall into this trap. Jesus confronted evil directly, but not in any and every situation where he found himself. The other danger is to refuse to see evil at all and to seek *any* other explanation. It has been said that the devil's cleverest wile is to convince us that he does not exist. There are limits to therapeutic, political and social theories as ways of explaining what we find in this world. Sophistication can be another form of naivety.

The word 'evil' attaches to some things quite easily, such as child abuse, terrorism or war. We also stereotype evil. Hollywood villains are instantly recognisable by their sinister appearance and manic laugh: in a film, it is clear who is good and who is bad. This means we can maintain a respectable distance from a world where evil remains so destructively present. But our diagnosis does not go deep enough.

In his study of evil in human life, *The People of the Lie*, psychotherapist M. Scott Peck noted that what he most wanted to call 'evil' was not found in the mind or behaviour of the evidently extreme, disordered personalities. It was found among people who looked and sounded completely respectable and reasonable—until you realised what they were actually saying and doing.[24] Evil masquerades as light (2 Corinthians 11:14) and presents itself under the appearance of 'good'. The devil is described by Jesus as 'the father of lies' (John 8:44). Evil is an active resistance to what is true (hence the title of Dr Peck's book). It is a fundamental orientation to falsity.

In their baptism, Christians publicly make two very

serious commitments that flow from their commitment to follow Christ. They are asked, 'Do you reject the devil and all rebellion against God? and 'Do you renounce the deceit and corruption of evil?' Christian living includes a commitment to the active resistance of evil. When we pray, 'Deliver us from evil' in the Lord's Prayer, we are not asking for a private escape from this world. We are praying to be people who do not live the lie and are thus part of the turning of the world from falsity to truth.

I remember discussing this with a friend who was off work with chronic back pain. At the time, he was employed by an international publishing company whose approach to business and the treatment of employees was plainly ruthless. I remember saying to him. 'This is evil. You are working in a place whose values and behaviour are destructive of every Christian and human value.' We prayed, 'Deliver us from evil' and a sense of release followed. The naming of evil for what it was, was itself freeing and strengthening as my friend returned to work as a Christian in a corporate culture that many were finding unbearable.

So put on the *whole* armour of God, says Paul. Be *fully* equipped. The armour he describes—breastplate, shield, helmet and so on—covers a soldier's front. It acts as protection for what we are *facing*. In the presence of evil and its destructive grip on so much human living, Christian presence in the world is offensive.

FOR REFLECTION

Prayerfully imagine, or mime, putting on the armour of God (Ephesians 6:14–17), and take confidence in it.

HIDDEN AND REVEALED

HOLY LAUGHTER

As the first day of the week was dawning, Mary Magdalene and the other Mary went to see the tomb. And suddenly there was a great earthquake; for an angel of the Lord, descending from heaven, came and rolled back the stone and sat on it... The angel said to the women, 'Do not be afraid; I know that you are looking for Jesus who was crucified. He is not here; for he has been raised, as he said. Come, see the place where he lay. Then go quickly and tell his disciples, "He has been raised from the dead."'... So they left the tomb quickly with fear and great joy, and ran to tell his disciples.

MATTHEW 28:1–2, 5–8

Stories told too often can easily lose their capacity to surprise. We know them too well. So, when approaching the major seasons of the Christian faith, I pray for one insight or thought to come fresh to me. Last Easter it came in this story, with the angel who 'rolled back the stone and *sat on it*'—that detail. I can imagine that rolling a heavy stone away on your own would leave you out of breath but I never considered it might be a problem for angels.

Sitting down has a 'job done' feel to it. It is the way we picture Jesus at the right hand of God. Certainly, while the angel is sitting on it, there is no chance that anyone could roll the stone back again. The mood feels teasingly casual, somehow. Something solid enough to seal in death itself is reduced to a handy spot to sit for a moment.

We surely do not suppose that the stone was rolled away to let Jesus out. If death could not hold him, a stone would be no obstacle. Rather, it was rolled away to let us *in*. There is a discovery for us to make. I fancy the angel fixing me with a mischievous 'You won't believe what I've just seen!' smile. Actually, this morning I think he winked at me! I am trying to pray but I keep giggling.

There is a literary theory that all storytelling revolves around four types of plot, which correspond to the seasons of creation: autumn is tragedy, winter is satire, summer is romance and spring is comedy. Resurrection is a sign of spring-time. New life is emerging after the long death of winter, and this is the season of comedy.

It may be that our most trusting response to the resurrection story is laughter. Let the lawyers and theologians do the serious analysis, but do not miss the angel sitting on that stone watching us all, grinning. How did the angels in the tomb contain themselves, waiting for the first bewildered witnesses. 'Shh, they're coming!' Well, wouldn't you, on a day like that?

The poet Anne Sexton was often left bruised in her pilgrimage through faith and life, but in one of her most moving poems she imagines meeting up with God, who surprises her by producing a pack of cards and playing poker with her. She is dealt a hand, as, in a sense, we all are in this life. We make what we can of what we find in our grasp. To her surprise, it is a very strong hand. She thinks she has won. Then God trumps her with a fifth ace! He cheats—he breaks the rules—but her response is not outrage. She loves it! The poem ends with the poet and God doubled over each other in helpless laughter at their 'double triumphs'.[25]

I once invited a prayer group to silently imagine they were entering the court of God the king. They were to draw near with whatever expressions of reverence they felt appropriate. The mood was serious until someone suddenly laughed out loud. I asked afterwards what had happened. 'Well, you know when you are in the presence of someone really important, you feel awkward and tongue-tied and they say something to relax you?'

'Yes,' I said.'

'Well, God told me a joke.'

There is an important tradition, in many older societies, of the clown or jester. In royal courts, among religious dignitaries and in the marketplaces, they have permission to mock the pomposity of the powerful and dethrone the self-important. They laugh at the po-faced solemnity that we confuse with reverence. They simply refuse to take us seriously—and that is their gift. Their laughter relativises the powers. They roll large and important stones away and just sit on them.

This is the season of comedy. Resurrection is God's fifth ace. He has broken the rules. You just have to laugh, don't you?

PRAYER

Lord, teach me to trust enough to laugh.

BUILDING PLANS

To the exiles… May grace and peace be yours in abundance… Come to him, a living stone, though rejected by mortals yet chosen and precious in God's sight, and like living stones, let yourselves be built into a spiritual house, to be a holy priesthood… For it stands in scripture: 'See, I am laying in Zion a stone, a cornerstone chosen and precious; and whoever believes in him will not be put to shame.' To you then who believe, he is precious; but for those who do not believe, 'The stone that the builders rejected has become the very head of the corner.'

1 PETER 1:1–2; 2:4–7

It takes a moment to realise what strange teaching this is. To urge people to build with material that has been rejected by professional builders as flawed and unsuitable for the task is not only foolish, it is surely dangerous. But, says Peter, God does exactly that. This is bizarre—complete nonsense.

It is very possible that Peter had a particular stone in mind. Like all cities in the ancient world, Jerusalem was surrounded by quarries that supplied the never-ending demand for building stone. As the quarrymen cut into the hillsides, faults in the rock face would be exposed, perhaps the result of earthquakes back in time. As this rock was unusable, they would simply dig around it to find a purer seam behind. Over time, the floor of the quarry would be littered with stumps and blocks of flawed stone, standing isolated, exactly where they were found and rejected by the builders.

We know of one such stone, in a quarry by the side of one of the main roads into Jerusalem. In the time of Peter, the locals had nicknamed it 'The Skull', perhaps because there was a suggestion of the shape of a head and face in it. It was also a place of execution. Somewhere near this stone, Jesus was crucified (Matthew 27:33).

Peter would surely have had a secondary meaning in mind, too. He could not write about stones without this meaning coming to his mind, because, in Greek, 'Peter' is the word for stone, and Jesus, the rejected stone, had said to him, 'You are Peter, and on this rock (*petra*) I will build my church' (Matthew 16:18). Peter knew all too well that he was a flawed stone himself.

There is evidence that, in the earliest years of the church in Jerusalem, Christians worshipped beside that stone each Easter Day. Imagine what a powerful and inspirational memory this would have been for them. Peter is drawing on this memory as he writes his letter to those he calls the 'exiles'—small, widely scattered communities of believers about whom we know almost nothing. That huge region, which today includes Turkey and areas beyond, was populated mostly by subsistence tenant farmers with no legal rights or voice. They were disenfranchised resident aliens. Such people knew what it is to be found flawed, treated as of no worth and left behind.

To such people comes this unexpected invitation; it is to them he is writing. 'Come to Jesus,' he says. 'You too are like stones in the quarry, left behind like so much debris— odd shapes and flawed pieces that no one has found any use for. You were discarded after the powers had made their choice according to their own measures of life and importance, but you are, in fact, of great value. You are like living stones in a temple being built to God's glory. Your lives are a holy offering, not a source of shame.' Recalling the image of the magnificent temple in Jerusalem, Peter even calls them priests. This is all as startling as it is bold.

We too are living stones. We are also flawed, unpromising and left far behind when judged by the preoccupations of this present age. But listen! All the usual measures of what makes us acceptable, impressive or even useful have been suspended—or, rather, reversed. Something quite new is going on here. 'Come to him,' says Peter. Really? This takes some trusting. We should expect a church built on such a foundation to look foolish, sound irrelevant and be easy to mock and despise. We will never be impressive building materials—but nor was Jesus. He was a stone the builders rejected. If Jesus, the rejected one, is the foundation stone of life, we are being shown a completely new way of knowing ourselves and of seeing and knowing God. All that has been rejected and left behind as worthless must be seen in a new light.

So here we find ourselves. Beyond all probability, we are living stones in a building that no one thought wise or possible.

FOR REFLECTION

I offer myself, flawed and unsure as I am, to be part of what Christ is building.

DO NOT JUDGE

'Do not judge, so that you may not be judged. For with the judgement you make you will be judged, and the measure you give will be the measure you get.'

MATTHEW 7:1–2

I will make a number of judgements today—some large, some small, some routine and some more significant. Responsible work and living requires it. I am also a Christian. Following Jesus calls me to make tough choices about my values, priorities and actions. When Jesus says, 'Do not judge', he does not mean abandoning all these necessary thoughts. What concerns him here is not 'making judgements' so much as the consequences of living with a judgemental spirit.

The psychotherapist Adam Phillips tells of a man who came to him seeking help with his decision-making.[26] In fact, the client gave every appearance of being someone who was totally clear about what he wanted and how to achieve it (even making plain to Phillips precisely what he wanted from the counselling sessions). He seemed to be a man in a hurry. He expected answers to his questions quickly and directly. It was no surprise to hear that when he was out with friends, they complained that he walked so fast, they couldn't keep up. He was the kind of person who, when presented with a menu in a restaurant, would make his selection in seconds, shut the menu and then sit with undisguised impatience as the others at his table took their time discussing and pondering the choices on offer. He was a man of strong, final judgements.

Phillips shrewdly suggests that, far from being decisive about what he wanted, the reality was actually the opposite. The man's responses were symptoms of deep anxiety. He lived in fear of uncertainty and therefore of managing choices. By quickly foreclosing decisions, even about what he wanted to eat, he was avoiding the space where he would have to face real dilemmas and real possibilities. Phillips finds in this story a parable of much contemporary living. He suggests that we use consumer choice (and *any* choice will do) to avoid living with real choice.

We judge like this when our anxieties drive our responses to life, and, if security is what we need, then being 'religious' and committed to God offers more attractive options than most. We look very principled and moral. Those firm assumptions about right and wrong, good and bad, feel very reassuring. We know where we stand and so do others. But this is the same exercise in avoidance. It is simply a bid for control, and the people around us will experience it as such, for it invariably becomes a judgemental, negative, policing interference in the lives and choices of others.

Nothing frustrated Jesus more than encountering a life that was shaped around a judging spirit. Jesus was constantly confronted by religious devotion that had become narrow, mean, excluding and loveless. It angered him even more when it was presumed to reflect what God was like and what was therefore required of his followers. Notice that Jesus does not say, 'If you judge, God will punish you by judging back.' In fact, he doesn't mention God at all. The focus is on us. Quite simply, this kind of living rebounds on those living it. We get back what we give out, in the same measure. Try to judge life, and life will judge you. Try to control life, and you will end up with a life that controls you.

'Do not judge' sounds like a succinct summary of Phillips' diagnosis of his client's needs. If Jesus had approached that table in the restaurant, where the menu was already firmly closed, and said to the man, 'Do not judge', how would he have reacted? Would he have been uncomprehending, or perhaps unsettled? After all, his whole world was carefully shaped to avoid precisely this kind of challenge. There were signs that, at some deeper level, he knew his need: why else was he seeking counselling? But he didn't stay long, apparently. 'He wanted me to make him a better decision maker,' Phillips comments on reflection. 'I wanted to help him to be a better risk taker.'

So why do we do it? Why do we limit our choices so quickly (and religiously) when so much more is on offer? What is it we fear about the wide, unfixed 'menu' of the life that Jesus invites us to?

Do not judge life, says Jesus. Just don't do it. Say 'yes' to life—and it will say 'yes' to you.

FOR REFLECTION
Yes!

TIME ENOUGH

For everything there is a season, and a time for every matter under heaven:

> *a time to be born, and a time to die;*
> *a time to plant, and a time to pluck up what is planted;*
> *a time to kill, and a time to heal;*
> *a time to break down, and a time to build up;*
> *a time to weep, and a time to laugh;*
> *a time to mourn, and a time to dance...*
> *a time to seek, and a time to lose...*

I have seen the business that God has given to everyone to be busy with. He has made everything suitable for its time... God has done this, so that all should stand in awe before him.

ECCLESIASTES 3:1–4, 6, 10–11, 14

The list goes on and on. All of life is there. There is a time for *everything*. This is more than a catalogue of chance or predictable events that tend to happen through life, some good, some bad. The writer calls them (literally) 'seasons', the word we use to speak of the purposeful rhythms and cycles of life.

Each season of creation has its distinctive tasks and priorities. Autumn's work is not the same as summer's. Winter is not to be judged for not being spring. The faithful work of each season enables all the others. But I wonder if winter ever feels guilty for lacking the vitality and colour of summer. Does spring feel shallow and activist as it looks at the unhurried depths and fruitfulness of autumn?

The same is true of our human seasons of life. Each season has its place, calling and potential. Each brings its own gift and cost. Each has its own dignity and beauty. Each comes with particular tasks and poses particular challenges, and we must be willing to live in them *all*. Trying to live in a world of permanent summer productivity is unsustainable and leaves us dis-eased. The saying goes, 'What cannot be avoided must be welcomed'. A life that welcomes every season will require an acceptance on our part (for we did not choose it), our reconciliation to it (for those element of it that we would not have chosen), our willingness to nurture it, and a reverence for it (because, however strange, it is a gift found in God).

How would you describe the present season of your life? What challenges does it pose for you? What are its gifts and opportunities? What is its cost?

Some seasons are predictable. We speak of stages in life, including childhood, education, relationships and home-making, ageing and retirement. My experience, though, is that just because I know a stage is coming, it does not mean I am prepared for everything it requires of me when it arrives.

Other seasons are neither expected nor desired. A sudden redundancy or bereavement can tip a life that was thriving on the fresh energy of spring into deep winter. A friend is emerging from a serious health scare. He has had the all-clear and has returned to life and work, but he is finding that his priorities have changed. He is no longer interested in working the way he worked previously. Nothing matters in quite the same way. However, he does not want to lose the subversive freshness that this experience has brought into the routines that have shaped his living for so long, so the frightening crisis has brought unexpected gifts. It is posing new challenges to life and faith. There is no way back to 'normal'; he is not the same person. It's the season.

To embrace life's seasons requires a trusting relationship with time. Why? Because God 'has made everything suitable for its time' (3:11). 'Suitable' is an unhelpful word for what is meant here. It is much more than just being useful or fit for purpose: the NIV's 'beautiful' is better. Everything is 'beautiful in its time', says Ecclesiastes, because all of life is the work of God.

So much of our relationship with time is anxious. We argue and fight with it. The supposed lack of time is one of the miseries of our age. Our resources for daily living are preoccupied with finding ways of doing things more quickly and so 'saving' time. The writer of Ecclesiastes would call this kind of living 'vanity' (1:2, literally 'empty'). It is a waste of time.

We need another place to start from.

Time is God-given.

God allows time to be time.

Time is not working against us.

Time gives life its direction and priorities.

All finds its beauty in its time.

Thank God for time.

PRAYER

Lord, teach me, in the present season of my life, to embrace its gift, to be faithful to its calling and to discover its beauty.

THE EYE OF THE STORM

The word of the Lord came to him, saying, 'What are you doing here, Elijah?' He answered, 'I have been very zealous for the Lord, the God of hosts; for the Israelites have forsaken your covenant, thrown down your altars, and killed your prophets with the sword. I alone am left, and they are seeking my life, to take it away.' He said, 'Go out and stand on the mountain before the Lord, for the Lord is about to pass by.' Now there was a great wind, so strong that it was splitting mountains and breaking rocks in pieces before the Lord, but the Lord was not in the wind; and after the wind an earthquake, but the Lord was not in the earthquake; and after the earthquake a fire, but the Lord was not in the fire; and after the fire a sound of sheer silence. When Elijah heard it, he wrapped his face in his mantle and went out and stood at the entrance of the cave.

1 KINGS 19:9–13

I am writing during one of those times when the news from around the world is full of unspeakable suffering and violence—and all too much of it in the name of God. 'People never do evil so completely and cheerfully as when they do it from a religious conviction,' wrote the 17th-century French philosopher, Pascal.[27] On Facebook last week I stared, unprepared, at a harrowing photograph of victims of brutal death. I wept helplessly. The image burned in my imagination for days. I hated those who had done it.

I find hard questions of faith surfacing at such times as these. How do we live, pray and believe in such a world, without tipping into despair and exhaustion, or without simply adding our own angry and vengeful responses to the behaviour of those we condemn?

Elijah lived in violent and turbulent times (indeed, he participated in the violence in no small measure), but we meet him sheltering in a cave in the Sinai Peninsula, on the holy mountain of God's own revelation. He is exhausted, angry and despairing of life: 'Lord, they have thrown down your altars and killed your prophets with the sword… I alone am left, and they are seeking my life.' There are many in refugee camps, hiding in caves, trapped in the ruins of their homes or wandering on desert roads who understand this feeling all too well. It has been so since the beginning: 'For your sake we are being killed all day long; we are accounted as sheep to be slaughtered' (Romans 8:36).

There in his mountain exile, Elijah finds that God answers no questions and takes no sides. Nor does he offer much comfort. He has already asked a question of his own: 'What are you doing here, Elijah?' And Elijah has responded defensively, out of his own fear and need. God now stages a drama. A massive whirlwind comes by, but the Lord is not in the whirlwind. Next an earthquake, but God is not in that, either. Last comes fire, but that is empty too. These natural phenomena are all familiar to God's people as symbols of God's supreme revelation and power, as Elijah knows well. But although they may accompany God's presence, they are not to be confused with his actual presence. Here they are all empty.

But then comes—what exactly? 'Sheer silence'. No one knows quite how to translate those words. Now God's question comes again. A truer translation might be, 'What is there here for you, Elijah?'[28] Elijah's journey was from the mountain of his powerful achievements for God (on Mount Carmel), to the mountain of God—from thunder and fire to this silent, divine 'nothing'. His faith must be recentred outside all human measures of presence, power and significance. What is here for him? Just God.

I find an insight here. We too need to come to such a place. We too may need rest. Like Elijah, we need to lay down the burdens of faith and work, to be deeply recentred, if we are not to despair. I have heard this described as 'seeking the eye of the storm'. The 'eye of the storm' is the name given to the place of unexpected calm at the centre of cyclones. It is a helpful image because faith is not an escape from a difficult world. It is a way of being present in the midst of it. In the heart of the storms, with whatever we grasp of the world's anguish, we wait in the 'sheer silence'.

And what is here for us? Just God.

PRAYER

Teach me, Lord, in this midst of this world's anguish, to find the eye of the storm.

ON NOT KNOWING

When I was a child, I spoke like a child, I thought like a child, I reasoned like a child; when I became an adult, I put an end to childish ways. For now we see in a mirror, dimly, but then we will see face to face. Now I know only in part; then I will know fully, even as I have been fully known.

1 CORINTHIANS 13:11–12

'We don't yet see things clearly. We're squinting in a fog, peering through a mist,' says verse 12 in *THE MESSAGE*. It comes as a surprise to find Paul talking of his faith in such terms. It is certainly not language that would inspire confidence in leaders of churches or organisations today, but perhaps we should ask ourselves why.

A significant corner of my working life involves accompanying individuals on their journeys of life, faith and prayer. This is traditionally called 'spiritual direction'. I notice one recurring feature of these occasions, especially when meeting with someone for the first time. As they share their story, a familiar anxiety stirs within me. In a moment they will stop talking. They will expect me to respond wisely, but I do not know what to say. I have no answer to their situation! Counsellors describe the same experience. While I am sitting there consumed by anxieties about my own skills and performance, I have stopped listening completely, and if I respond out of those insecurities, the conversation will be manipulated around me and my needs. What is required is a willingness to enter the *not*-knowing, to be willing *not* to understand. I must be willing to go peering through the mist with the individual, surrendering any need of mine to be the 'solution'.

A tribute paid to the pioneering child psychiatrist Donald Winnicott was about his 'monumental capacity to contain *un*knowing'. He was open to the not yet understood or revealed. I see a similar challenge in the Christian church at this time. Facing decline and indifference in the society where it once had a central place, the pressure to find the answers and solutions that will turn the tide is enormous—but the challenge is the same. We must first develop a capacity for not-knowing.

In her timely book *Learning to Walk in the Dark*,[29] Barbara Brown Taylor notes how we speak of faith by using opposites—light and darkness, sacred and secular, true and false, and so on. In each pairing, the first element named is presumed to be the nearer to God. The result is the pursuit of what she calls 'full solar spirituality'—faith lived in the constant, unclouded light of God's presence. Much Christian belief assumes this to be the goal, and so darkness becomes the image of doubt or failure of faith. It is where evil and sin hide and do their worst work. We fear the dark, avoid it and pray for God to lighten it. Darkness has little or no positive place in faith and prayer. Curiously, this mirrors the surrounding culture, where, with our endless reliance on technological aids for every part of life (including computer screens and phones), we have little experience of actual darkness. There is growing evidence of the damaging effect of this 'light pollution' on human health. It is simply bad for us to live only in the light. We are missing the dark.

Brown Taylor argues that faith needs 'lunar spirituality' for its faith and health. Lunar spirituality welcomes the dark in the journey of faith and does not immediately reach for the light switch when darkness comes. Darkness actually expands our vision and sensitivity: we see much further at night. Without regular sight of that vast wilderness above us, we are impoverished and fall prey to strange assumptions about ourselves. Darkness also helps to interpret the light. Every artist knows how closely dark and shade must work with light if a face or scene is to be revealed in its fullness and depth. The mystics speak of a dazzling darkness which is actually an *excess* of light—just as we are blinded by looking straight at the sun. This is the darkness of the overwhelming nearness of God's brilliance, not his absence.

The dim, foggy vision of which Paul speaks is not the failure of faith. Rather, it flows from faith. It may even be our greater witness to this world that we do *not* know or see clearly. Our testimony is not to what we know. It is to the mystery of a vision and purpose for this world that is God's alone. To live there, our capacity for unknowing must be infinite.

PRAYER

Lord, help me to deepen my capacity to contain unknowing and to walk in the dark with you.

WITH UNVEILED FACE

All of us, with unveiled faces, seeing the glory of the Lord as though reflected in a mirror, are being transformed into the same image from one degree of glory to another; for this comes from the Lord, the Spirit... For it is the God who said, 'Let light shine out of darkness', who has shone in our hearts to give the light of the knowledge of the glory of God in the face of Jesus Christ.

2 CORINTHIANS 3:18; 4:6

When did you first discover you had a face? This is not a trick question. Was it when you first saw your reflection in something? How did you know that what was gazing back at you was *you*? Or was it in a photograph? These can horribly distort our image. 'That looks nothing like me!' we often protest.

Answer: you first discovered you had a face when someone gave you theirs. One of my favourite photographs is of my son, one day old, just after his first bath. He is lying on a towel and, from out of the corner of the picture, my wife is bending her face close to his. He is gazing intently at her; they are meeting face to face. In time, he began to reach out and touch what he saw, explore its features and begin to make connections with the unseen contours that he would come to know as his own face.

We have known for some time just how important the gift of a face is for each of us. We need it to be true, or true enough, to give us the purchase we need, a secure attachment, from which to start our own journey across the terrain of the life into which we have just been born.

At this point, our contemporary culture presents us with a particular dilemma, for which face do we trust? There is no single image on offer; the choice is overwhelming. So whose likeness do I seek? Which image do I adopt? How we look, who we look like, are matters of enormous concern. At stake is our whole sense of who we are, and of knowing ourselves to be loved, accepted and valued. An entire consumer economy is structured around finding new ways to stimulate these anxieties. The cost to us is huge, and unless we can keep up, we simply lose face.

Theologian Jane Williams puts it well:

Our faces become a series of masks that we try on and discard, always searching for the real 'me', always looking for the face that will make others love us or fear us, masks that make us powerful, invulnerable, beautiful, feared, acceptable, some that we don't even know that they are just masks, and all the time getting further and further away from the face we were made to mirror, the face of Jesus. The irony is that without these masks, we are made in the image of God.[30]

Into such a world, Christianity comes as a religion of faces. It does not begin with a philosophical thesis or a creed to assent to, but in the turning of one face to another. In today's passage, Paul speaks of it as an unveiling. 'All of us, with unveiled faces...' Really? Does anyone remember this unveiling taking place? We were being so careful to preserve our masks. Who unveiled our faces?

Jesus did. It is him coming down to us, meeting our face with his.

You know those times when, in the middle of a crowd, someone's face looks familiar? We walk on thinking, 'I'm sure I know that person from somewhere.' C.S. Lewis suggests that the moment we finally see the face of Jesus will be such a time. We will know that we have always known him, for he was present in every loving turning we made to one another, however fleeting.[31]

It is all mutual, this vulnerable disclosing. We turn to God and find him turned to us. In the face of Christ, God reveals his own image, and, in coming to us in our own likeness, he reveals our own true face to us. He is giving us back to ourselves. A lost image is being restored.

In all committed relationships there is a vulnerable journey involved—living under the loving gaze of another, daring to trust ourselves as being loved and accepted for who we are, learning to live without masks. The journey of faith is no different. We are held in the steady, secure gaze of one whose love is true. The first response of prayer is simply to return the gaze—just that. There is no longer any need to hide.

FOR REFLECTION AND PRAYER

'Come,' my heart says, 'seek his face!' Your face, Lord, do I seek. (Psalm 27:8)

HABITS, REFLEXES AND RESPONSES

YOU HAVE DIED

Do you not know that all of us who have been baptized into Christ Jesus were baptised into his death? Therefore we have been buried with him by baptism into death, so that, just as Christ was raised from the dead by the glory of the Father, so we too might walk in newness of life… If we have died with Christ, we believe that we will also live with him… So you also must consider yourselves dead to sin and alive to God in Christ Jesus.

ROMANS 6:3–4, 8, 11

A wise older friend once shared how he would begin his prayers each day by affirming that he was a child of God and then imagining himself going down into the waters of baptism, submerged with Jesus, leaving his old self behind and emerging to new life, named and embraced in the delight of the Father's love. I was surprised, because he was a deeply spiritual man. While I was only too aware of the weakness of my own faith, I did not imagine him needing to repeat a prayer like that. I now know that Christian living is a journey of continual, repeated remembering. 'Do you not know?' Yes I do, but I keep forgetting.

Baptism marks the entry into Christian life. The word means 'immersion' but the drama is expressed in different ways. Symbolic sprinkling is the way in many churches. In some parts of the world, a river is used. Some churches hire the local swimming pool. The baptised enter from one side and go under the water, to emerge to a new life on the other. There, like all newborns, they are embraced, named (traditionally, this would have been a new name, a 'Christian' name), clothed and fed. However and wherever it happens, Paul reminds us that baptism is an actual participation in an event of utterly life-changing power.

The exodus story in the background to Paul's imagery here. This is easy for today's readers to miss, but the connection is made explicitly in the Christian baptism service as the water is blessed: 'Through water you led the children of Israel from slavery in Egypt to freedom in the promised land.' The Israelites' journey from a life of slavery and death to a new life was through the waters of the Red Sea. They emerged on the other side as a new people. Old ways of living no longer had power over them, although their journey into that truth would take longer, as it does for us.

There is no resurrection without dying. It is resurrection *from* the dead, not somehow bypassing death. We must die to ourselves, enter the waters and be buried with Christ. Some believers can remember a particular time and place where they did this, but for everyone it is a commitment that is revisited and renewed with every challenge that life brings. It may come as some relief, laying down the burden of old, sterile ways of living that we could not change, but it may also involve struggles with old weaknesses or deep fears.

I have never forgotten an experience the night before I was to be ordained. Quite unexpectedly, I plunged into deep terror at what I was about to do. All was darkness; God was absent. I felt I was at the end of my life. But the next day I stood in the cathedral feeling so overwhelmed with awe that I am still not sure how I remained standing. That evening, in front of the community where I was to begin my ministry, I was asked how it all felt. I replied that I was not sure if I was at a funeral or a wedding! Baptism is both. What I was facing was anxiety about ordination. It was the meaning of my own baptism—to die, to be buried in Christ. 'Do you not know?'

This raises questions about a common way of expressing Christian conversion—accepting or receiving Jesus into 'my life'. Paul's language here flows in the opposite direction. I am immersed into the death and resurrection of Jesus. Jesus receives me into *his* life. Strictly speaking, there is no longer a 'me' to receive him at all, for I have died and been buried with him and raised with him to a new life. If the focus remains on 'me', I will tend to be also focused on 'my' faith, and that is a recipe for anxiety. We are the last people we should be trusting for our salvation. Our faith is not in *our* faith now. We have died. Our faith is in Christ, and it is completely safe in him. We have been given another life, one that is truly our own.

PRAYER

Lord, please lead me through death to life.

HATING

Large crowds were travelling with him; and he turned and said to them, 'Whoever comes to me and does not hate father and mother, wife and children, brothers and sisters, yes, and even life itself, cannot be my disciple.

LUKE 14:25–26

What are we to make of this teaching? On the face of it, it is a complete contradiction of all that we assume to be Christian behaviour. Like many, I spend my life trying to avoid such responses within me, not permit them. The gospel is about loving, not hating, isn't it? So hatred must be something to turn away from, not towards. But not only does Jesus command us to hate, he tells us to direct that hatred at our nearest and dearest. Unless we hate *them*, says Jesus, we cannot be his followers.

Jesus often taught in a style, popular in his day, that used extreme statements or cartoon-like opposites to emphasise a point. The effect was often funny and was certainly not all to be taken literally. Christians don't actually cut off 'offending' body parts as a way of dealing with sin (Mark 9:43–45). Nor do we have physically huge planks of wood sticking out of our eyes, that we are unaware of as we helpfully point out to others the 'specks' of their minor failings (Luke 6:41–42). The purpose of this style of teaching was to shock the hearers into a new awareness. Well, there is no chance of missing the shock here, and the message is utterly serious.

We need to understand the context of Jesus' teaching. The society of his day was organised around closed structures of belonging. In such a culture, loyalty was shown first to your family and to those in its extended networks. When it came to career, business contracts, social influence and privileges, family and friends were favoured ahead of others, regardless of ability or merit. Those who did not belong to any group or clan were simply left out. This is called nepotism and it still exists in many forms today.

What Jesus hated about these closed family-based worlds of self-interest was that they destroyed the possibility of having a society based on justice, equality, inclusion, generosity and compassion. Accidents of birth, privileged connections through education, being born a man rather than a woman or living in parts of the world that can command food and resources at the expense of those in other parts—all this, Jesus says, is to be hated passionately. We are to hate it for the sake of the love we meet in Christ, who came to establish a new community beyond the discriminating privileges of birth, race, tribe, gender and social status.

The late Trevor Huddleston, who campaigned tirelessly against apartheid long before the cause became popular in the West, once startled a group of trainee ministers by declaring, 'I want to impress on you the importance of learning to hate! We have forgotten how to hate. We must hate what is evil.' To an audience more accustomed to repenting of such an emotion, this was disturbing, to say the least.

Jesus' teaching reminds us that our stronger emotions

are not problems to be tamed or somehow got rid of. The real problem is not that we have powerful and disturbing emotions; it is that they don't do what they are meant to do. They need converting. We are to direct our capacity for anger and hatred against sin, injustice and evil, and Jesus teaches that the battle is nearer to home than we realise.

This probably sounds unsettling and risky. If we have been accustomed to managing our stronger feelings at a distance, entering the love of Christ and the life of the Spirit will be marked at times by a disturbing loss of emotional balance. We worry about 'losing our tempers'. It may be that we have yet to find them in the first place! The gospel is much more than a remedy for our weaknesses. It is, more importantly, concerned with the conversion of our strengths. Christian faith is an *off*ensive, not defensive, presence in this world.

The hatred to which Jesus calls us is not the opposite of love. It is love rightly directed, passionately opposed to all that destroys, obstructs or undermines his radical community of welcome and justice. It is evil that we hate, not the people who are caught up in evil.

To live and work passionately for such a world, we will need all the energies that God has created within us. We will not have strength for the task without them. That is why learning to hate is so essential—and why the poet William Blake wrote of seeking the form of heaven with the energy of hell.[32]

PRAYER

Jesus, help me only to hate what you hate, out of the love with which you love.

REJOICING

Rejoice in the Lord always; again I will say, Rejoice. Let your gentleness be known to everyone. The Lord is near. Do not worry about anything, but in everything by prayer and supplication with thanksgiving let your requests be made known to God. And the peace of God, which surpasses all understanding, will guard your hearts and your minds in Christ Jesus.

PHILIPPIANS 4:4–7

Christian joy is not a feeling that comes when life is going right (although we are grateful when it does). It is not based on material circumstances—quite the opposite. The striking thing is how often it is found among those for whom life is far from kind or good. Christian joy has a way of surfacing in the most unlikely circumstances, so it is present as a sign of contradiction.

The man writing the words in today's reading was in prison for his faith. His name was Paul, and the people he was addressing were vulnerable and struggling with the circumstances they were facing. Yet joy runs right through the heart of this letter. Why rejoice? 'The Lord is near.' What else do we need to know? For Paul, joy is nothing less than the presence of Jesus. It is therefore faith in action.

During the Communist era in Eastern Europe, a Lutheran

pastor called Richard Wurmbrand spent 14 years in Romanian prisons for his faith. Often in solitary confinement, frequently tortured, hungry and in poor health, he kept faith alive by reciting Bible passages from memory. He tells of his response to the teaching of Jesus in Luke 6:22–23: 'Blessed are you when people hate you, and when they exclude you, revile you, and defame you on account of the Son of Man. Rejoice on that day and leap for joy.' Wurmbrand duly rejoiced, but then stopped and challenged himself: 'I have only carried out half this command. Jesus clearly says we must leap.'

There in his damp, cramped underground cell, tubercular and in rags, he began jumping for joy. A passing guard saw this strange sight. Perhaps concerned that his prisoner was having a breakdown, he wandered off and returned to toss a hunk of bread into the cell. Wurmbrand then remembered the rest of the verse:

'Rejoice and leap for joy—for behold your reward is great'!
It was a very large piece of bread—more than a week's rations.
I rarely allowed a night to pass without dancing, from then on.
Though I was never paid for it again.[33]

Christian joy is, first of all, an encounter with Jesus and his love. Joy reveals the character of God. In the words of Pope Francis, 'Our Christian joy drinks of the wellspring of [Jesus'] brimming heart.'[34] Christian rejoicing is not, as it might seem, an attempt to spiritualise or ignore the reality of suffering and injustice. Quite the reverse: it is a work of resistance. Joy subverts the temporal realities and mocks their claims. It insists, despite all the evidence, on the celebration of a different story. Joy is a work of faithful defiance. It is faith on the offensive.

Christian joy radically refocuses the world and our experience in it. It breaks though our narrow preoccupations by widening our vision. Rejoicing in the Lord decentres us and our concerns. We find ourselves held, in trusting faith, in the emergence of a far greater story.

Rejoicing takes practice, and there is little in the world that prepares us for this. It needs to be exercised so that it becomes a faithful reflex. Recalling his prison cell, Wurmbrand writes, 'I found that joy can be acquired like a habit. I learned to rejoice in the worst conditions.'[35] Such a response may be hard to make: there will be times when the struggles of life may make rejoicing difficult or even impossible. To demand rejoicing when life seems impossible sounds insensitive and even abusive, but, in the Bible, the prayers and protests of those struggling with life are wholly part of the community of faith, too. Paul's 'rejoice' is an encouragement to trust, not a demand to be happy. When life is painful and God seems absent, the response of joy, if we can make it, may feel like a sacrifice (Hebrews 13:15).

Finally, Christian joy in this age is always an anticipation of the future. Even Jesus found strength in this, for we read that 'for the sake of the joy that was set before him [he] endured the cross' (Hebrews 12:2). Beyond all deserving, in defiance of any and all circumstances, there is something about Christian joy that touches eternity.

FOR REFLECTION

Rejoice and leap for joy—and if this is too difficult, why not just practise for when you can?

CONFESSING

If we say that we have no sin, we deceive ourselves, and the truth is not in us. If we confess our sins, he who is faithful and just will forgive us our sins and cleanse us from all unrighteousness.
1 JOHN 1:8–9

The pronouncements of a British Prime Minister were once satirised by tweaking a word in this verse: 'If we say we have no *spin*, we deceive ourselves.' It was a time of controversy over the way the national government was communicating information to the public. 'Spin' is when the reporting of events is manipulated to disguise bad news by placing a (dubiously) positive interpretation upon it. Spin is therefore a refusal to be truthful and accountable. It flatters to deceive.

When we define sin as wrong doing or wrong thinking, we easily trivialise it. Our diagnosis does not go deep enough. Who we are comes before what we do. The sin we call 'original' in the creation story was not the theft of fruit from God's orchard. The first human beings were seduced into believing that 'when you eat of [the fruit]… you will be like God' (Genesis 3:4). This was a bid for a world other than what is given—a refusal to accept their own creatureliness and to honour God's own 'Godness'. The irony is that they were attempting to steal what was already given. They were already in God's image, in paradise, but in the attempt to possess it they lost the original gift, too. It all collapsed. They lost God, lost each other, lost their world and lost their own selves. Sin is, thus, an orientation to falsehood. It is the pursuit of a life that is not real because it is not the life that is given.

This means that even repentance is not something we can achieve for ourselves. We must pray for what we seek. 'Grant us true repentance' is a line from an ancient prayer. We can only receive it as a gift of God. Notice the word 'true'. This is pastorally wise: guilt and shame are not always reliable guides to what needs confessing as sin. Likewise, our motives are complex and contradictory. They are all part of what needs redeeming in us. I can be deeply sorry—when it suits me to be. Being penitent can feel very pious while actually being a refined form of spiritual showing off. Crocodile tears are not real. We can spin it all, actually, and even our best intentions cannot save us.

Christian faith is often accused of being morbidly obsessed with sin (and this chapter may be confirming that impression so far). That can certainly be a tendency, but to be obsessed with sin—just as to trivialise it—succeeds only in encouraging us to avoid God. The central message of Christian faith is not that we are sinners but that we are *forgiven* sinners. The mark of true repentance is not sorrow for sin, but the *break* with sin. The focus is on God, not us. The old Christian word for what we need is 'compunction'. Compunction describes a particular work of the Spirit, not something we can do for ourselves. The word shares the same root as 'to puncture'. Picture a large, inflated balloon. It has the appearance of fullness but is actually empty. In the same way, our lives can have the appearance of substance while being the opposite. We speak of people having inflated opinions of themselves. Compunction is what happens when a pin is taken to a balloon: what was inflated is pierced. There was no substance; the truth was not in us.

The Bible uses a variety of ways to speak of God, humanity and sin. One of the more familiar borrows from the world of law courts and criminal justice to explore guilt, justice and punishment. Today's passage speaks of a work of 'cleansing'. The word recalls the ritual purity required in temple worship, but it might also remind us of the compassion with which Jesus drew near to the marginalised, excluded and broken people whom the world of his day called 'sinners'. He welcomed and embraced them with such love and touched them so tenderly. The work of cleansing, disinfecting, binding and restoring to health is one of gentleness and understanding.

Jesus is the friend of sinners (Matthew 11:19). God's greatest revelation of himself is in the place of our sin, so, if we say have no sin, we miss it all. He meets us here, with love that is truthful, that does not deceive us, that forgives and cleanses us. 'Only the sinner understands the gospel,' wrote Richard Holloway, 'for only the sinner knows their need of it.'[36]

PRAYER

Lord, help me to come to true repentance.

HALLOWING

'Pray then in this way: Our Father in heaven, hallowed be your name.'

MATTHEW 6:9

What does it mean to 'hallow'? What are we praying for? Sports enthusiasts speak in hushed tones of the 'hallowed turf of Wembley'. A person 'of hallowed memory' is being named with particular affection and respect.

In its deepest sense, to hallow is to honour and love another *for their own sake*. When a couple pledge in marriage to love each other 'for better or for worse', that is a commitment to hallowing. It is love offered beyond any notion of transaction, exchange or contract. Hallowing is gratuitous—an honouring offered freely, without condition, charge, measure or any thought of self-interest or personal gain.

'Hallowing' is not an everyday word. Some versions of the Lord's Prayer suggest 'honour' as an alternative, but this could mean little more than 'respect'. Something more is needed. In other versions, the prayer is for God's name to be 'made holy', but 'making holy' is not something we can do for God. Only God can hallow, for only God is holy. Either way, a society organised around consumption and competition, in which everything is valued for its worth or profitability, will struggle to make any sense of this word at all.

By contrast, the 'Hallowing of the Name' (Hebrew: *Kiddush ha-shem*) is central to Jewish and biblical faith. It sums up the whole business of life and is found in its most costly and stubborn expression in the midst of pain and tragedy. The story of Job is a good example. It begins in the heavenly court, where Satan is in conversation with God.[37] God boasts to Satan of how faithful Job is to him, but Satan points out that God has blessed Job so generously that this faithfulness is really not surprising. Satan asks, 'Does Job love God for nothing?' (literally 'as a gift': Job 1:9), and so the drama begins. Job has been faithful to God while his life has been blessed, but is this really love or just shrewd bargaining? What will happen if life goes ill for him? The test of hallowing comes precisely when there is nothing to be gained from it.

The story is told of a Holocaust survivor whose family and many more known to him died in the extermination camps. Surveying the tragedy in his life, he tells God that he knows what is going on: God wants him to give up believing in him. But this he simply refuses to do: 'No, no, a thousand times no! For you and against you, this song you shall not still!' he says.[38]

As the prophet Habakkuk endured a world in which any visible sign of blessing or the goodness of God had vanished, he still affirmed, 'Yet I will rejoice in the Lord; I will exult in the God of my salvation' (Habakkuk 3:18). There are also times in the Bible when God's people protest at their suffering and God's apparent neglect of them, but their concern is not for themselves but for the way their situation reflects badly upon God and his name. Through all of life, in fullness and in emptiness, God is to be hallowed for the sake of his own name.

The twelfth-century saint Bernard of Clairvaux taught that there are four movements in the life of faith. We begin by loving ourselves for our own sake. Then, when faith awakens, we love God, but still for our own sake, as one who blesses us and meets our needs. Thirdly, we must come to the love of God for God's own sake—as gift, for nothing, for the hallowing of the divine name alone.

Bernard then identifies one more movement. It is too easily missed, though perhaps with the best of intentions. In the loving of God for God's own sake, we come to love *ourselves* truly for God's sake. There is no contradiction here. God is the life of heaven and earth: it is all sustained in the love that is God's own being. When his name is truly hallowed, all things find their true place, hallowed in their own name and calling.

So we pray those ancient words once more: 'Hallowed be your name'. And, did we imagine it? The echo of the prayer returns to us: 'Hallowed be *your* name'.

FOR REFLECTION

Do I love for nothing?

BELONGING

Ruth clung to her… [and] said,

> 'Do not press me to leave you
> or to turn back from following you!
> Where you go, I will go;
> where you lodge, I will lodge;
> your people shall be my people,
> and your God my God.
> Where you die, I will die—there will I be buried.
> May the Lord do thus and so to me, and more as well,
> if even death parts me from you!'

When Naomi saw that she was determined to go with her, she said no more to her.

RUTH 1:14, 16–18

These beautiful words are often read at weddings, where they express the joyful mutuality of shared love. They were first spoken, though, in the context of bitterness and loss, and they were not welcomed. Ruth's offer was initially refused. The background to this story of exile and tragedy was summarised in an earlier reflection (Thursday of Week 1). This reading rejoins the story as the widowed Naomi wants only to return to her home and community, to die. Her two widowed daughters-in-law are not of her nationality. One returns to her own people, and Naomi urges the other, Ruth, to do the same. These words are Ruth's reply.

Ruth is a person who, beyond all prevailing wisdom or common sense, refuses to accept divisions, so her story is a challenging illustration of the cost and gift of 'belonging'. Her commitment breaches all boundaries of belonging. By the end of the story, Ruth, an outsider, is to be found at the heart of a community alive with new hope, and has become the mother of a family line from which Israel's greatest king, David, will trace his descent.

By her actions, Ruth challenges social assumptions and norms about relationships. In a culture where all security and worth were bound up in marriage, Ruth (literally) 'cleaves' to Naomi. The word expresses a powerful bonding: in the Genesis creation story, it describes the marriage bond (Genesis 2:24). In 'cleaving' to Naomi, Ruth pledges commitment beyond the traditional norms of marriage.

Ruth also refuses to be separated by racial and ethnic divisions: 'Your people shall be my people.' What future can a Moabite widow hope to have in Israel? It is not hard to imagine parallels around the world today. But, by her decision, Ruth becomes the point of connection in the story that unfolds. People like Ruth are 'bridge' people, who cross the divides and so become the means by which others cross and meet each other. Every society needs its bridge people, those who bring together what is separated. Strangers may then become friends, and fear may become trust.

Ruth also refuses religious divisions: 'Your God will be my God.' We do not know what has persuaded Ruth to make such a pledge without any word, promise or sign of blessing from a deity who has treated Naomi so badly, but she is making her own journey of faith across another of the most violent divisions in today's world.

Finally, although Naomi never thanks her for it, Ruth's commitment to her becomes a means of healing. When life has left us broken or desperate and beyond hope, we need others who can hope for us and, initially, just stay with us. Ruth does this for Naomi. There on the trail, Naomi sees that she is determined and gives in. They begin the journey in silence. For the moment, all that needs saying has been said.

There comes a point in the Communion service, as the community prepares to share bread and wine, when many churches share what is called 'a sign of peace'. With varying degrees of formality, people turn, reach out and greet each other with words such as 'The peace of the Lord be always with you'. It is a holy moment, in which we are doing much more than agreeing that we have things in common or that we like each other. Our faith calls us to reach out to each other across all that may divide us.

We are to be a community without boundaries. We are to be bridge people and so become places of meeting, relating and healing. This requires a determined cleaving to each other, beyond our well-guarded frontiers of nationality, class, faith or friendship, and at times we may find ourselves unwelcome and pushed away.

Ruth's story reminds us that when we greet neighbour or stranger in 'the Peace', we are saying much more than 'I am your friend'. We are saying, 'I cleave to you in Christ—come what may.'

FOR REFLECTION

What might such a commitment ask of me beyond my own community and networks?

SATURDAY PEOPLE

How long, O Lord? Will you forget me for ever?
How long will you hide your face from me?
How long must I bear pain in my soul,
and have sorrow in my heart all day long?...
Consider and answer me, O Lord my God!
Give light to my eyes, or I will sleep the sleep of death...
But I trusted in your steadfast love;
my heart shall rejoice in your salvation.
I will sing to the Lord,
because he has dealt bountifully with me.

PSALM 13:1–3, 5–6

Today is Saturday (if you are reading this book in its daily
sequence, that is, which is not obligatory). By choice, it is
the day in the week when we like to relax, away from work.
In Jewish and biblical faith, Saturday is the day of rest—the
sabbath. When you can choose, how do you spend a day like
this?

There is another Saturday—not one in which we choose
to spend time, but one that occupies an important place in
all our human living. It is the Saturday between Good Friday
and Easter Day, between the cross of Jesus and his resurrection. This day symbolises all those waiting spaces where we

find ourselves living between promise and fulfilment, losing and finding, death and life. All of us arrive at this day at some time or other. For some, the journey with it is long and painful; others must learn to make their home there.

Donald Eadie is a pastor, preacher and social campaigner who also lives with a chronic physical disability. Out of personal necessity and through long engagement with the stories of others, he has reflected deeply on the experience of those he calls 'Saturday people'.[39]

The community of Saturday people is very varied. It includes, for example, those living with serious illness or long-term, life-restricting disabilities, and those who accompany them. Victims of social exclusion, prejudice and deprivation are also found here. Saturday people may be those living through unsettling change in their lives, where outcomes are uncertain—unemployment, life losses and other transitions. This is a community of all faiths and none, with no quick solutions on offer. The challenge to religion is to resist resorting to superficial comforts or easy answers.

There are no maps at hand for Saturday people. This is a place of waiting, and little in our culture prepares us for the challenge when it comes. Eadie notes that the sustenance we need in this place is of a very different kind, like a deeply rooted plant drawing what it needs from hidden depths. We usually have a clear idea of what we are waiting for— clear wishes and actual outcomes in mind—but for Saturday people the waiting must be open-ended. It is a waiting beyond the waiting, where outcomes are neither clear nor predictable and we have to lose control. Open-ended living requires a surrender, an act of trust and a willingness to be shaped by 'something that is far beyond our own imaginings'.[40] We do not come to it easily.

Whose company are you sharing on this Saturday? Roger is a friend who has lived for years with chronic health issues and is frequently near to death. Chris is on a harrowing journey through the break-up of his marriage. Sue is there too, somehow sustaining faith in a church so conflicted about sexuality that she must keep a fundamental part of her identity and selfhood hidden. Ann lived with multiple sclerosis for 43 years. In terms of her most basic need, God worked no miracles for Ann, but her husband John recalls how often, though lacking speech and (latterly) movement, people seemed changed by the experience of meeting her. Something was given and received, outside any familiar measures of human exchange. 'Perhaps she ministers to God,' he mused.[41]

Jesus is also found among the Saturday people. In the accounts of his earthly ministry, his authority and power are often noted, but, as he approaches his final suffering and death, Jesus is described in passive mode. He is 'handed over' to other authorities. He follows where once he led. He is now acted upon. In the words of the Apostles' Creed, he 'suffered under Pontius Pilate, was crucified, died and was buried'. On the Saturday between his cross and resurrection, death and life, we meet him here, with all who wait.

PRAYER

Lord, help me to stop trying to be in control and, instead, to wait in openness and trust for the future you will bring.

WEEK 6

IN THE SHADOW OF THE CROSS

CHOOSING FREEDOM

For freedom Christ has set us free. Stand firm, therefore, and do not submit again to a yoke of slavery... For you were called to freedom, brothers and sisters; only do not use your freedom as an opportunity for self-indulgence, but through love become slaves to one another.
GALATIANS 5:1, 13

From their nest under the eaves of our holiday villa, three baby swallows noisily clamoured for food as their parents flew far and wide to meet the endless demand. While we were there, the time came for them to fly. You could see the growing restlessness and the instinct to flex and stretch their wings in the crowded nest. Two of them in quick succession took off, swooping across the sky with increasing confidence. The third stayed in the nest, occasionally perching on the edge but then drawing back. Several more days passed before it too opened its wings and trusted itself to the air and the environment for which it was made. Of course, we knew how it felt. Life is just such a series of challenges to choose, to risk and to 'let go'.

'If the Son makes you free, you will be free indeed,' said Jesus (John 8:36). He spoke of his life as a way of freedom and he was never more scathing than when condemning the burden of religion shaped around loveless rule-keeping. So why does Paul have to keep challenging the earliest Christian communities to guard their freedom and not regress back into what he calls 'slavery'? What is the attraction of a life or religion that enslaves us, anyway? There is no shortage of it around. Anyone with experience of church life will know how communities that outwardly sing and proclaim the freedom of God's love can be deeply conservative, resistant to change and highly dependent in practice. The problem is not that slavery is attractive; there is something in freedom that we fear more.

There is a saying, 'as free as a bird'. Human beings have always looked with envy at the beauty of a bird in flight. If only nothing constrained or weighed us down, we too could live freely, we suppose. That is the popular definition of freedom. The trouble is, no such world exists; this is actually the desire for a life in which we have to take no responsibilities. And while we are unable or unwilling to exercise choice over the way we live, we are more likely to become enslaved to the various forms of addictive and compulsive behaviour that are now endemic in our society. The philosopher Immanuel Kant noted how, when a bird opens its wings to fly, it encounters the air as resistance. The bird might be tempted to conclude that it could fly a lot more freely without it—but without resistance it would be unable to fly at all. This is the paradox. Freedom comes only to those who are prepared to meet resistance.

We are not born free. We must learn freedom, and we all start from very different places. A gymnast knows only too well that their apparently effortless freedom is the result of endless practice. For a person with fragile self-esteem, their confidence crushed by their experiences of life, the invitation to freedom will be received vulnerably, and the response will take real courage. But Christian freedom is not a demand; it is a gift. Jesus knows what it asks of us and what we need to let go, in order to embrace it. His love is patient and he makes the journey with us (Matthew 28:20).

Religion does not always help at this point. It can have a way of confusing faith with passive dependence on God, which can look and sound very pious but is actually a way of avoiding responsibility. There is a freedom that even God would not take from us. Theologian Karl Rahner expressed the challenge of faith in this way: 'I would like to be a person who is free and who understands and shows by his actions that he is at the mercy of his freedom, a freedom which throughout his life is creating and making him finally who he should be... a person who is faithful, who loves, who is responsible.'[42]

Freedom is the practice of obedience. This is not the contradiction it sounds, for to be free is to be living in complete obedience to the environment for which we were made. That environment is the love of God. The freedom he gives us is to become the people he has truly made us to be. That is what lies behind the striking affirmation about God in an ancient prayer for peace—a God 'whose service is perfect freedom'.[43]

PRAYER

Lord, teach me to serve you with my freedom.

WHY THIS WASTE?

Six days before the Passover Jesus came to Bethany, the home of Lazarus, whom he had raised from the dead. There they gave a dinner for him. Martha served, and Lazarus was one of those at the table with him. Mary took a pound of costly perfume made of pure nard, anointed Jesus' feet, and wiped them with her hair. The house was filled with the fragrance of the perfume. But Judas Iscariot, one of his disciples (the one who was about to betray him), said, 'Why was this perfume not sold for three hundred denarii and the money given to the poor?' (He said this not because he cared about the poor, but because he was a thief; he kept the common purse and used to steal what was put into it.) Jesus said, 'Leave her alone. She bought it so that she might keep it for the day of my burial.'

JOHN 12:1–7

The beginning of the week that leads to his cross finds Jesus at the house of Mary, Martha and Lazarus—three friends and a home very dear to him. Just days before he hosts a last Passover meal for his disciples, some of his disciples host a meal for him. As he anticipates his own death (we learn later that the plots to kill him, and Lazarus, are common knowledge), he is sitting and eating with someone recently raised from death. John 12:1 is the only place where Lazarus is named first, and apart from his sisters. The Eastern

Orthodox Church celebrate his story from death to life on the day before Palm Sunday: they call it 'Lazarus Saturday'. For Jesus at that meal, and for his followers since, the way of suffering and the cross begins with a story of one who has been raised from the dead.

At some point in the evening, Mary unexpectedly produces half a litre of very high-quality aromatic oil and anoints the feet of Jesus. The pungent fragrance would have been overwhelming for everyone present. Her action provokes an argument, quite possibly triggered by embarrassment, for it was public and very intimate within that culture.

Parallels with the last supper continue, for Judas is present. (Lest we should miss his role as betrayer, it is spelled out in brackets in verse 4). Judas criticises Mary's action as wasteful (v. 5; see also Matthew 26:8)—and what she did was certainly a startling extravagance. The oil would have cost a year's wages. John bluntly questions Judas' motives in pointing this out (v. 6), while Jesus silences Judas and affirms what Mary has done, linking it to his own death.

Unlike the last supper, this occasion will not end in betrayal. Nor is Jesus left alone with his burden while his uncomprehending disciples fall asleep or deny him. Instead, one disciple seems to have understood. Mary drew near and ministered to him without any regard for the cost to herself. She anointed him for his own 'passing over'.

'Why this *generosity*?' might be a more accurate question than 'Why this waste?' In the background is the approaching demonstration of crucified love, beyond any measure or costing. Excessive generosity was a feature of so much of Jesus' ministry and teaching, starting with the very first miracle, when he turned water into huge qualities of wine at a wedding (John 2:1–11). That miracle is described by

John as the 'arch sign' (v. 11, literally)—and what is it a sign of? That God is immeasurably, ridiculously, unreasonably generous. It is not enough to miraculously feed more than 5000 people: twelve whole basketsful are left over (Matthew 14:20). When you fish with Jesus, the boat is likely to sink with the weight of the catch (Luke 5:7). And what of all those parables of lavish feasts and banquets, at which the least deserving takes the honoured place (see Luke 14:11)?

Why this waste? Because this is how God loves. Divine love has no interest in restricting itself to what is 'necessary'. It is no use looking to the events of this coming week for a proportionate, costed response to the needs of the world. It is not means-tested, not tied to productivity or deserving.

The generous sacrifice of Jesus cannot be summed up in sober moral equations or legal judgements. God's love is simply not sensible like that. It is beyond measure, poured out in overwhelming excess over an ungrateful, uncomprehending world. Mary knew this. In her gift to Jesus, she mirrored the wastefulness of God. She was loving as God is loving. Her love was poured out like God's and for God, beyond thought of cost and beyond any notion of what is sensible.

PRAYER

Jesus, may all my living reflect your extravagant, wasteful love, and may those whose paths I cross catch just a little of the fragrance of your presence.

OUTSIDE THE CITY

Now the chief priests and the whole council were looking for false testimony against Jesus so that they might put him to death, but they found none, though many false witnesses came forward. At last two came forward and said, 'This fellow said, "I am able to destroy the temple of God and to build it in three days."' The high priest stood up and said, 'Have you no answer? What is it that they testify against you?' But Jesus was silent. Then the high priest said to him, 'I put you under oath before the living God, tell us if you are the Messiah, the Son of God.' Jesus said to him, 'You have said so. But I tell you, From now on you will see the Son of Man seated at the right hand of Power and coming on the clouds of heaven.' Then the high priest tore his clothes and said, 'He has blasphemed! Why do we still need witnesses? You have now heard his blasphemy. What is your verdict?' They answered, 'He deserves death.'

MATTHEW 26:59–66

The trial of Jesus was an appalling miscarriage of justice. The verdict was predetermined and the 'evidence' was manipulated. Witnesses perjured themselves. Legal processes were compromised. Religious leadership was being driven by personal hatred, with a defensive religious institution manipulating theology. Fear of reputation was driving policy outcomes, so moral responsibility was abandoned as political expediency replaced justice. An innocent man was condemned to death and a convicted murderer released in his place (Matthew 27:21–22). Finally, the Roman governor famously washed his hands of Jesus (v. 24)—but responsibility is one thing that leaders cannot avoid. There he is, named also in the creeds that Christians have recited down history ever since: 'crucified under Pontius Pilate'.

If the leaders come out of this story badly, the followers fare no better. Groups and individuals are found acting out of fear and self-preservation, abandoning their beliefs and their friends to save themselves. Followers disown, deny and betray Jesus, some 'only obeying orders' while others are just going along with the crowd. The force of public opinion and threats of violence tie the hands of those in authority, leaving them with an impossible task. To be a follower is to be no less responsible.

Religion comes out of this story no better than politics. The death of Jesus was the work of devout, God-focused people. When the stakes are high, and deep securities are threatened, religious people may not fight fairer than anyone else. On the eve of his ordination, a young man received this advice from an older priest: 'If you are to be a priest in the church, you need almost as high a doctrine of corruption as you do of glory.' I do not think that is a cynical conviction. There is a dark side to believing as to everything else—perhaps more so, since 'the faithful' presume to be acting with divine sanction. A faith with a cross at its centre is well aware that it is part of this world's deadly capacity for self-delusion and evil.

When God is put on trial and condemned to death by his own creation—God killed in the name of God—you know that something is desperately wrong. So how did this story become the 'good news' that Christians have proclaimed to the world ever since? Here it is: the cross of Jesus reveals God's saving love for the world.

The first Christians reflected on all this in the context of the sacrificial system in the Jerusalem temple. There, offerings of unblemished animals were made as atonement for the sin of the people. The blood was poured out in symbolic expression of it, and the carcasses, now unclean, were destroyed outside the city. The parallels were obvious. Jesus too was a pure offering of innocent blood: 'Jesus also suffered outside the city gate in order to sanctify the people by his own blood' (Hebrews 13:12). 'Outside' represented the place of ultimate rejection of all that was thought to be beyond the will, blessing or presence of a holy God—but there, outside, is Jesus.

What happens when a religious sacrificial system, based on the management of sin, guilt and debt, receives a perfect victim who makes a free gift of their life for what they do not owe? The whole system collapses. It is rendered redundant, no longer the basis of our acceptance or forgiveness. If divine love meets us in the gift of Jesus on the cross, there is nowhere that is outside God's blessing and embrace. 'Let us then go to him outside…' (Hebrews 13:13).

PRAYER

Lord upon the cross, nowhere is outside your love. Help me to live in this world in the light of that truth.

TAKE UP YOUR CROSS

Then he began to teach them that the Son of Man must undergo
great suffering, and be rejected by the elders, the chief priests, and
the scribes, and be killed, and after three days rise again. He said all
this quite openly. And Peter took him aside and began to rebuke him.
But turning and looking at his disciples, he rebuked Peter and said,
'Get behind me, Satan! For you are setting your mind not on divine
things but on human things.' He called the crowd with his disciples,
and said to them, 'If any want to become my followers, let them deny
themselves and take up their cross and follow me. For those who
want to save their life will lose it, and those who lose their life for my
sake, and for the sake of the gospel, will save it. For what will it profit
them to gain the whole world and forfeit their life?'

MARK 8:31–36

Jesus never hid from his followers what his ministry was
leading towards. For their part, his disciples never stopped
struggling to accept and make sense of what he was saying.
He tells them once again, and on this occasion Peter feels
he has heard enough. Suffering, rejection, defeat and being
killed are surely not what should happen to real Messiahs?
Nothing in the faith they have grown up with has prepared
them for this idea, so he takes Jesus to one side and bluntly
tells him he is wrong.

This is startling language. Elsewhere, the word 'rebuke' is used to describe Jesus' response to demons (for example, Matthew 17:18, Mark 1:25; 9:25). But Peter's behaviour here may well owe more to fear than presumption, for, if Jesus' words are true, then they, his disciples, could also be in danger. Peter expresses what they are all thinking, and Jesus is looking at them all as he interrupts Peter: 'Peter, get out of my way! Satan, get lost! You have no idea how God works' (v. 33, *THE MESSAGE*).

Not only is there no other way for Jesus, but the way of the cross, that utter surrender to what the Father wills, is the way of his followers too. This is an uncompromising image of faith. Carrying a cross is the action of someone on the way from their cell to the place of execution. In American prisons, inmates on death row used to say 'dead man walking' when one of their number made that last journey. What life-plans, hopes and ambitions make any sense at all in that moment?

To take up our cross is to surrender all attempts to use life, religion and God for our own ends and needs—but the instinct to make such attempts runs very deep. Something of this is happening whenever we choose which church to join or which styles of preaching or worship we prefer, and there is no lack of types of spirituality and meditation on offer that are little more than therapeutic comforts. It may all look admirably devout and spiritual, but our peril is that we are engaging in activities that are powerless to save. We cannot save ourselves.

At a Christian gathering, someone was once inspired to speak words as from God: 'I have no other way to offer you than the way of my Son.' To be honest, my heart sank on hearing this message. It felt too challenging and costly at that moment. I could well understand the disciples who found

Jesus' teaching so hard that a number of them left him. He turned to those remaining and asked them if they were leaving, too. Peter replied, 'Lord, to whom can we go? You have the words of eternal life' (John 6:68). Where else is there, indeed? But we get the feeling that they would have been grateful to find something less costly on offer.

The story is told of a man seen, late one night, searching for something under a streetlight. A passerby stops and asks, 'Did you lose something here?' 'No, I lost it over there,' replies the man, pointing into the darkness some distance away, 'but the light is much better here.' His folly is plain. He has lost something important and knows it. He is looking hard for it, but he is searching on his own terms and, while he does so, he has no hope of finding what is lost.

To take up our cross is to set our mind on 'divine things', says Jesus. This all hinges on God and what he is about. All our hope is found here, for the cross is for ever the sign of a God who loves, saves, delivers and raises life out of the darkness of what is dead and lost.

Those who lose their life here will find it.

PRAYER

Nothing in my hand I bring,
Simply to your cross I cling.
FROM 'ROCK OF AGES' BY AUGUSTUS TOPLADY (1725)

DO YOU UNDERSTAND WHAT I HAVE DONE?

Jesus knew that his hour had come… During supper Jesus, knowing that the Father had given all things into his hands, and that he had come from God and was going to God, got up from the table, took off his outer robe, and tied a towel around himself. Then he poured water into a basin and began to wash the disciples' feet… He came to Simon Peter, who… said to him, 'You will never wash my feet.' Jesus answered, 'Unless I wash you, you have no share with me.' Simon Peter said to him, 'Lord, not my feet only but also my hands and my head!'… After he had washed their feet… he said to them, 'Do you know what I have done to you?… If I, your Lord and Teacher, have washed your feet, you also ought to wash one another's feet… Very truly, I tell you, servants are not greater than their master, nor are messengers greater than the one who sent them. If you know these things, you are blessed if you do them.'
JOHN 13:1–6, 8–9, 12, 14, 16–17

'Do you know what I have done to you?'

Well, no, not without some help. Washing feet is not a social ritual in Western culture. I can imagine that, in a hot climate, the washing of bare or sandalled feet was a refreshing and hygienic provision after the dirt and dust of the journey. It also expressed respect and honour for guests when they arrived at your home, but, in my world, such respect does not extend much further than putting a clean towel by the handbasin. This kind of washing is something we do for ourselves. It is private. 'Do you mind if I use your bathroom?' 'Of course—at the top of the stairs, first door on the left.'

What are we supposed to understand by this action of Jesus? John sets the scene very carefully. The hour has come (in John's Gospel, specific references to time are always about what God is up to, not about us, and 'the hour' is always about the cross). All is completely prepared. (In other accounts, the room itself has been booked ahead for the meal.) Jesus himself is acting out of a full sense of who he is, where he has come from, where he is going, and what he is called to do. It is all in his hands.

In the light of this, Jesus now acts, and here the story takes an unexpected turn. He 'lays down' (v. 4, literally) his outer robes, puts on a towel and washes his disciples' feet.

Foot-washing was usually done by a servant or by the youngest member of the household. We know from other accounts of this meal that the disciples got into an argument about which of them the greatest (Luke 22:24), and this may be why. The issue was not about who was greatest; no one wanted to be the *least*. But then Jesus, their Lord and leader, washed their feet.

'Do you know what I have done to you?' Jesus' actions are carefully described. As already mentioned, it begins with a laying down of his outer robe—and this is where the whole story has begun. Jesus is the one who laid down the glory of heaven, emptied himself and chose the place of a servant in this world (see Philippians 2:7).

'Do you know what I have done for you?' 'Laying down' has a further association. The text uses the same Greek word that, not long before, describes the good shepherd who 'lays down' his life for his sheep (John 10:11).

'Do you know what I have done for you?' If you take off the outer covering, whatever has been concealed is now revealed: the secret is laid bare. Divine love is humble. It is a way of life in which all is laid down for the love and service of the other. There is no competition, no pecking order or hierarchy. Jesus is giving us a glimpse of heaven.

'Do you know what I have done to you?' If we want to see Jesus, we must look down, not up. He is there kneeling at our feet, washing them. This is a washing we cannot do for ourselves. We must surrender to being 'done to'; grace must embarrass us. All is prepared for us. This is the only love on offer and it is always found beneath our dignity, beneath our feet, unashamed in the mess, the dirt.

Do we understand? This is to be our way of life, too. It is the way of all blessing.

FOR REFLECTION

I imagine Jesus speaking this question to me: 'Do you understand what I have done for you?' What is my response?

WHEN GOD IS TORN FROM GOD

From noon on, darkness came over the whole land until three in the afternoon. And about three o'clock Jesus cried with a loud voice, 'Eli, Eli, lema sabachthani?' that is, 'My God, my God, why have you forsaken me?' When some of the bystanders heard it, they said, 'This man is calling for Elijah.' At once one of them ran and got a sponge, filled it with sour wine, put it on a stick, and gave it to him to drink... Then Jesus cried again with a loud voice and breathed his last... Now when the centurion and those with him, who were keeping watch over Jesus, saw the earthquake and what took place, they were terrified and said, 'Truly this man was God's Son!' Many women were also there, looking on from a distance.

MATTHEW 27:45–48, 50, 54–55

The ministry of Jesus began, as he was baptised in the River Jordan, with the Father's cry of love from heaven: 'You are my Son, the Beloved' (Mark 1:11). It ends with that beloved Son crying out in agonised separation. After a life lived in a constant trusting intimacy with his *abba*, Father, Jesus prays here to 'God'. It is still a cry of faith—*my* God—but prayed from some unimaginably anguished distance.

How are we to understand what is happening here? A familiar telling of it focuses on sin, debt and judgement in a particular way. As if in court, humanity stands guilty of sin.

The sentence is death, and God's honour demands justice. But on the cross the innocent Jesus takes our place, pays all debt, takes the punishment and restores us to God. One of the difficulties with this summary is what it teaches about the relationship of the Father and the Son. Jesus taught, 'The Father and I are one' (John 10:30) and 'Whoever has seen me has seen the Father' (14:9). But do we meet, in Jesus, a God so concerned for his honour that he requires such a price for its restoring? There is another way of understanding this. The Father is not acting through the Son on the cross; he is acting *in* him. The cross is something they share and suffer together.

Jesus' cry is a quotation of the first line from Psalm 22. In Jewish faith, to quote the first verse of a psalm is to invoke the whole of it. It begins with the terrible desolation of being where God is not, crying out day and night but receiving no answer (v. 2). But the psalmist has not lost faith. God can be trusted: 'In you our ancestors trusted... and you delivered them... Since my mother bore me you have been my God' (vv. 4, 10). He tells of his present persecution and extreme physical suffering: 'I am... scorned by others, and despised... All my bones are out of joint... and my tongue sticks to my jaws' (vv. 6, 14–15). He casts himself on God: 'O Lord, do not be far away! O my help, come quickly to my aid!' (v. 19)

The the psalm speaks as if from the future, as if looking back at what is happening. It calls us to have faith: 'Praise him!... He did not hide his face from me... Future generations will be told about the Lord, and proclaim his deliverance to a people yet unborn' (vv. 23–24, 30–31). God will save.

That cry of Jesus is ours. He is crying the cry of the world. 'Were you there when they crucified my Lord?' the old spiritual asks. Yes, we were—because Jesus was there, in our humanity, in our sin, in the terrible dislocation of it all. God is calling to God from the farthest reaches of a God-lost world. To make that cry takes him to his very last breath.

That cry means there is nowhere where God is not. Jane Williams puts it like this:

> God is torn apart from God. This is the only kind of language we can find to express what seems to be happening. On the cross, God endures the separation from God that is ours. As Jesus cries, 'My God, my God, why have you forsaken me?' he is the life of God, streaming into our separation. Because Jesus and his Father are ripped apart, nothing can now separate us from the love of God in Christ Jesus. God is in our dislocation from God, as in our connectedness.[44]

Here, like the women, we must stand and watch and wait.

It is out of our hands. It is out of the hands of Jesus, too. It is abandoned into the hands of God.

FOR REFLECTION

I imagine myself standing at the foot of the cross of Jesus. Is there anything I want to say or ask?

DESCENDING TO THE DEAD

The women… saw the tomb and how his body was laid. Then they returned, and prepared spices and ointments. On the sabbath they rested according to the commandment.
LUKE 23:55–56

Christ also died for sins once for all… in order to bring us to God. He was put to death in the flesh, but made alive in the spirit, in which also he went and made a proclamation to the spirits in prison, who formerly did not obey.
 1 PETER 3:18–20

If this was a film, we would be watching the kind of setting you get the morning after a brutal battle has raged. In the first light of day, the camera draws slowly back and moves across a scene of smoky, tragic devastation. The music is reflective and haunting, the mood empty and hopeless.

After all the hectic and harrowing events of the last few days, the story has slowed right down. It is the Jewish sabbath. How hard this must have been for the women! They had not had time to finish preparing Jesus' body for burial before the sabbath started. The spices were ready; they surely longed for nothing more than to complete the work of honouring his remains and finally laying him to rest in the tomb, but they had to wait. Even the dead keep the sabbath. This delay can only have added to their pain, so soon after the anguish of watching him die.

What are we to do with this day? We do the same as the first disciples. We do nothing. That is the whole point. A body is lying dead in a tomb. It is the end. There is nothing we can do here. But this is Jesus in the tomb. Now, God cannot die, so whose body do you see there? Whose death is he dying? To seek Jesus on this day, we must contemplate our own end—see our own body lying there beyond breath, lifeless. That is where we meet him.

The Apostles' Creed declares, 'He was crucified, dead, and buried; he descended to the dead.' Holy curiosity (and more) has led to imaginative reflection as to where Jesus was on this day. What does 'descend' mean? The reference in 1 Peter 3:19 to Jesus going to the 'spirits in prison' adds to the mystery while stubbornly resisting attempts to clarify exactly what those words mean. Hidden beneath the surface calm of the sabbath, what is going on in the depths today?

Medieval imagination loved to picture Jesus descending to the world of the dead. He arrives at the gates of the underworld. Satan, whose kingdom this is, comes out to receive what he assumes to be the routine delivery of another human body due to him—for the penalty for sin is death. But he finds, to his utter horror, that he has received the sinless Lord of Glory into his domain. At a stroke, his kingdom is laid waste, evil is vanquished and death itself is defeated.

Another story is found in an ancient sermon written for preaching on the eve of Easter. It begins, 'Something strange is happening. There is a great silence on earth today because the King is asleep. God has died in the flesh and hell trembles with fear. He has gone to visit those who live in darkness and in the shadow of death. He has gone to free the captives, Adam and Eve.'

So it is that, in the unending shadowy gloom of lost paradise, Adam and Eve are found sitting among the dead. They look up, and there is Jesus! He stands before them, carrying his cross. He grasps them by the hand and says, 'Awake, sleeper, and rise from the dead, and Christ shall give you light' (Ephesians 5:14). He then preaches to them (at some length) before concluding, 'I did not create you to be a prisoner of hell... rise, let us leave this place. I am life itself. The banquet is ready.'[45]

There are ancient wall paintings and frescoes that vividly depict the moment when Christ rises from the depths, emerging with immense force, smashing to pieces the heavy tombstones that had, for so long, sealed death. There he stands, fierce and glorious in his victory, in full view of earth, the cosmos and all the heavens. Beneath his feet is the rubble that was once the underworld, hell's fortress, complete with smashed locks, broken chains and the last few demons fleeing in terror. And look! On either side of him, held firmly by their wrists, looking vaguely startled and dazzled by the brilliance of the new day, Adam and Eve have been raised with him!

PRAYER

Lord Jesus, please seek me too. Preach to me. Take me by the hand. Take me with you.

LOSING AND FINDING

Mary stood weeping outside the tomb. As she wept, she bent over to look into the tomb; and she saw two angels in white, sitting where the body of Jesus had been lying, one at the head and the other at the feet. They said to her, 'Woman, why are you weeping?' She said to them, 'They have taken away my Lord, and I do not know where they have laid him.' When she had said this, she turned round and saw Jesus standing there, but she did not know that it was Jesus. Jesus said to her, 'Woman, why are you weeping? For whom are you looking?' Supposing him to be the gardener, she said to him, 'Sir, if you have carried him away, tell me where you have laid him, and I will take him away.' Jesus said to her, 'Mary!' She turned and said to him in Hebrew, 'Rabbouni!' (which means Teacher). Jesus said to her, 'Do not hold on to me, because I have not yet ascended to the Father. But go to my brothers and say to them, "I am ascending to my Father and your Father, to my God and your God."' Mary Magdalene went and announced to the disciples, 'I have seen the Lord'; and she told them that he had said these things to her.

JOHN 20:11–18

Something happened in the night. Long before the first light of day, before anyone was around to witness it, before any human hand or faith could claim any involvement or revelation—God acted in the dark. Somewhere on the edge of the sleeping city is a garden with a tomb in it. The stone that sealed its entrance has been rolled away. The tomb is empty.

'The world has been breached by an enclave of non-death,' wrote Orthodox theologian Olivier Clément about that empty place at the heart of the Christian faith,[46] and there it waits to be discovered. (What God chooses to reveal or conceal is always a mystery to our human agendas.)

Mary finds it first. The tomb is empty, the body gone. Here in John's account she is alone. (The Gospels vary in emphasis and therefore detail. The men have come and gone home again in bewilderment.)

What is she to do? Grief-stricken and bewildered, she checks again. Now there are angels in there. 'Why are you weeping'? they ask. It is a strange question to ask someone standing by a grave. You would think the answer was obvious. Mary can only assume that the body has been stolen.

So it is that the first experience of resurrection is of loss and emptiness—but there is no other way. We will not come to it by any familiar ways of human understanding. Not for the first time, we encounter non-sense. Arguments for the resurrection suggest grounds for faith, but arguments cannot create faith. The empty tomb didn't convince the first disciples. Where was the body? It was yet another cruel twist in a story that had already left them frightened, traumatised and uncomprehending.

'Turning' is the key action in this story. It changes everything. Mary turns, away from the tomb. Someone is standing there, someone she knows so well but now does not recognise. 'Why are you weeping?' That question again. But faith comes to existence where it is needed most—in the very heart of our *in*comprehension and helplessness. This will be a familiar theme in the stories that follow. The risen Jesus is not to be recognised by human choice or will. It is for him to reveal himself. Faith is a gift. What is encouraging is that he is present even without our recognition.

There is a delightful irony in Mary's confusion. She was, in a way, quite right to think that Jesus was the gardener. Notice how John has set the scene: they are standing in a garden; it is the morning of the first day. Jesus is the new Adam; this is the beginning of a new creation, and Jesus begins, as the first creation began, by naming—'Mary'.

Now Mary turns again, but this time it is in astonished and joyful recognition. The world has been breached. Life streams through it. Christ is risen! Like Mary, we have only one journey to make. We must come to that place. We too must bend, look into the place of death and find it empty. That much we can do. And then, with our own mix of bewilderment, grief, searching and questioning, we must *turn*.

By ancient tradition, Christians renew the promise of their baptism of Easter Day: 'I turn to Christ.' And there he waits to greet us. He calls us by name.

FOR REFLECTION

Imagine that you, like Mary, are standing in the garden, facing the empty tomb. It is Easter Day. The risen Jesus is standing behind you. Make this your response of faith: 'I turn to Christ.'

QUESTIONS FOR GROUP DISCUSSION

Week 1: Becoming who I am

- What does 'the fear of the Lord' mean to you? Share the positive and negative associations of this phrase for you.
- Share ideas of what might constitute a 'sustainable rhythm of life' and how that might differ according to life circumstances.
- Discuss your experiences of prayer as complaint, lament or protest.

Week 2: The compass of our excitement

- How important for you is the receiving of Holy Communion? Can you articulate why it is—or why it is not?
- What resonances does the idea of 'wilderness' have for you, and why?
- Discuss your sense of what it means to call God 'Father', whether you find this a positive or negative concept, and why.

Week 3: In the midst of life

- What implications for faith does the scarred body of the risen Saviour suggest?
- If you had to identify yourself as an animal, which would you choose, and why?

- Imagine that Jesus is present at your group discussion. What question would you want to ask him, and what do you think his answer would be?

Week 4: Hidden and revealed

- What's your reaction to the idea of God the joker and God the rule-breaker?
- Reflect upon what 'season of life' you feel yourself to be in, and why. Share, as appropriate, with the group.
- What sort of masks can we end up wearing as Christians? How can we create churches where people are able to be themselves, without masks?

Week 5: Habits, reflexes and responses

- Discuss ways in which anger and hatred can actually be expressions of love and concern.
- Do you think it is harder to forgive or to feel forgiven, and why?
- Identify some practical ways in which you can be 'bridge people' in your local community.

Week 6: In the shadow of the cross

- How might you live out the costly obedience to God that daily life actually demands?
- To what extent does 'walking the way of the cross' feature in your own faith and in the worship and life of your church community?

■ Discuss the importance of 'silent waiting' on Holy Saturday in order to experience the full joy of Easter.

NOTES

1 Ellen Davis, *Proverbs, Ecclesiastes and the Song of Songs* (Westminster Bible Companion) (Westminster John Knox, 2010), p. 5. Davis cites E.F. Schumacher, *Guide for the Perplexed* (Harper and Row, 1977), pp. 55–56

2 Powers of Ten: www.youtube.com/watch?v=0fKBhvDjuy0

3 http://demellospirituality.com/awareness/37.html

4 http://www.catholicgkchestertonsociety.co.uk/Chesterton-s-Vision---on-Tv.html

5 Annie Dillard, *Teaching a Stone to Talk* (Harper and Row, 1982), p. 52

6 C.S. Lewis, *The Lion, the Witch and the Wardrobe* (Harper Collins, 1995), p. 75

7 David Whyte, *Crossing the Unknown Sea: Work and the shaping of identity* (Penguin, 2002), pp. 60–61

8 Paul Bradbury, *Life from Death Emerging* (Triangle, 2002), pp. 36–37

9 Adam Philips, *Missing Out: In praise of the lived life* (Penguin, 2013), p. xi

10 Michael Paul Gallagher, *Dive Deeper: The human poetry of faith* (DLT, 2001), p. 108

11 Kenneth Bailey, *Poet and Peasant and Through Peasant Eyes* (Eerdmans, 1985), pp. 180–182

12 *Common Worship: Services and Prayers for the Church of England* (Church House Publishing, 2000), p. 182

13 Angela Tilby in Fraser Watts (ed.), *Perspectives in Prayer* (SPCK, 2002), pp. 94–95

14 Jim Cotter, *Prayer at Night* (Cairns, 1986), p. 76

15 Cotter, *Prayer at Night*, p. 77

16 *Confessions* of St Augustine (III:6 and X:27), trans. Martin Laird, in *Into the Silent Land* (DLT, 2006), p. 8

17 Etty Hillesum, *An Interrupted Life: The diaries of Etty Hillesum, 1941–1943* (Pantheon, 1984), p. 9

18 Robert MacFarlane, *The Wild Places* (Granta, 2008), p. 203

19 Many commentaries use the word 'wise' to make the point that the serpent here is not the image of evil that words like 'cunning'

can imply to modern ears. See, for example, David Hill, *The Gospel of Matthew* (Eerdmans, 1981), p. 187

20 James Alison, *On Being Liked* (DLT, 2003), ch. 1 ('Contemplation in a world of violence')

21 'From Jerusalem to Jericho' (http://www3.nd.edu/~wcarbona/darley%20and%20batson%20-%20from%20jerusalem%20to%20jericho.pdf)

22 Chapter 53 of the Rule of Benedict: see Joan Chittister, *Wisdom Distilled from the Daily: Living the Rule of St Benedict today* (HarperSanFrancisco, 1991), p. 140

23 Chittister, *Wisdom Distilled from the Daily*, p. 141

24 M. Scott Peck, *People of the Lie* (Arrow, 1990)

25 'The rowing endeth' in *The Complete Poems* (Houghton Mifflin, 1982), pp. 473–74

26 Adam Phillips, *Houdini's Box: On the arts of escape* (Faber and Faber, 2001), pp. 112ff

27 Blaise Pascal, *Pensées* (Penguin Classics, 1995), para. 894

28 I owe this insight to Paula Gooder, writing in *Guidelines* (BRF, May–August 2009)

29 Barbara Brown Taylor, *Learning to Walk in the Dark* (Harper One, 2015)

30 Jane Williams, from an undated address

31 C.S. Lewis, *The Four Loves* (Collins, 2012), pp. 137–139

32 Blake explores this at length in *The Marriage of Heaven and Hell*. See *The Complete Works of William Blake* (Create Space Independent Publishing Platform, 2015)

33 Richard Wurmbrand, *In God's Underground* (Living Sacrifice Book Company, 2011), Kindle loc. 720

34 Pope Francis I, *Evangelii Gaudium* (The Joy of the Gospel), para. 5 (http://w2.vatican.va)

35 Wurmbrand, *In God's Underground*, Kindle loc. 721

36 Source unknown

37 In the story of Job, Satan is a member of God's heavenly court, where he has a role as a kind of prosecuting attorney, flushing out bad faith on earth. He is not to be confused here with the more common understanding of Satan as the devil, the arch-enemy of God.

38 Quoted in Gordon Mursell, *Prayer as Protest* (DLT, 1989), p. 168

39 Donald Eadie, *Grain in Winter* (Epworth, 1999), p. 6

40 Eadie, *Grain in Winter*, p. 10

41 John Goldingay, *Remembering Ann* (Piquant, 2011)

42 Karl Rahner, *The Practice of faith* (Crossroads, 1983), p. 3

43 Service of Evening Prayer, Book of Common Prayer

44 See www.fulcrum-anglican.org.uk/articles/the-holy-spirit-in-the-world

45 www.catholic.org/clife/lent/story.php?id=33117

46 Olivier Clément, *The Roots of Christian Mysticism* (New City, 1995), p. 55

ALSO FROM BRF

TRAVELLERS OF THE HEART

Exploring new pathways on our spiritual journey

MICHAEL MITTON

In this book one of the UK's leading authors on Christian spirituality and personal renewal shares his own faith journey, in the context of exploring some of the different spiritual traditions that have influenced Christian witness over the past 40 or so years.

Michael Mitton explores how encompassing something of the breadth of Christian spirituality, from Charismatic to Catholic, via Celtic, can not only enrich our faith but strengthen the mission of the Church.

ISBN 978 0 85746 221 3   £7.99

Available from your local Christian bookshop or direct from BRF: visit www.brfonline.org.uk

MENTORING FOR SPIRITUAL GROWTH

Sharing the journey of faith

TONY HORSFALL

In recent years the ancient Christian practice of spiritual direction has become increasingly popular, as more and more people from every part of the church seek to know God more deeply.

This accessible book is an introduction to spiritual mentoring, for those exploring this aspect of discipleship or embarking on training for ministry as a mentor within their church. As an experienced spiritual mentor, Tony Horsfall uses the metaphor of a journey to explain what mentoring means, its benefits to all involved, and how to explore the call to mentor others.

ISBN 978 1 84101 562 0   £6.99
Available from your local Christian bookshop or direct from BRF: visit www.brfonline.org.uk

DEEP CALLS TO DEEP

Spiritual formation in the hard places of life

TONY HORSFALL

The Psalms offer honest insights into the reality of life with God, reflecting every human emotion and situation. Through looking at some of the psalms written 'from the depths', we can understand more fully the way in which God is at work to shape our characters and form the life of Christ within us during difficult times.

Deep Calls to Deep will speak to those who are 'passing through the valley' but it will also be of help to anyone who desires a deeper walk with God, as well as those who accompany others on their Christian journey, as mentors, soul friends or spiritual directors.

ISBN 978 1 84101 731 0   £7.99
Available from your local Christian bookshop or direct from BRF:
visit www.brfonline.org.uk

ENJOYED READING THIS
LENT BOOK?

Did you know BRF publishes a new Lent and Advent book each year? All
our Lent and Advent books are designed with a daily printed Bible reading,
comment and reflection. Some can be used in groups and contain questions
which can be used in a study or reading group.

Previous Lent books have included:

The Way of the Desert, Andrew Watson
When You Pray, Joanna Collicutt
Welcoming the Way of the Cross, Barbara Mosse
Reflecting the Glory, Tom Wright

If you would like to be kept in touch with information about our
forthcoming Lent or Advent books, please complete the coupon below.

✂--

❑ Please keep me in touch by post with forthcoming Lent or Advent books
❑ Please email me with details about forthcoming Lent or Advent books

Email address: _____

Name _____

Address_____

_____

_____

Postcode_____

Telephone_____

Signature _____

**Please send this
completed form to:**

Freepost RRLH-JCYA-SZX
BRF, 15 The Chambers,
Vineyard, Abingdon,
OX14 3FE, United Kingdom

Tel. 01865 319700
Fax. 01865 319701
Email: enquiries@brf.org.uk

www.brf.org.uk

BRF is a Registered Charity

PROMO REF: END/LENT16

For more information, visit the **brf** website at **www.brf.org.uk**

Enjoyed

this book?

Write a review—we'd love to hear what you think.
Email: reviews@brf.org.uk

Keep up to date—receive details of our new books as they happen.
Sign up for email news and select your interest groups at:
www.brfonline.org.uk/findoutmore/

Follow us on Twitter @brfonline

By post—to receive new title information by post (UK only), complete
the form below and post to: BRF Mailing Lists, 15 The Chambers, Vineyard,
Abingdon, Oxfordshire, OX14 3FE

Your Details
Name _____
Address_____
_____
Town/City _____ Post Code _____
Email_____

Your Interest Groups (*Please tick as appropriate)	
☐ Advent/Lent	☐ Messy Church
☐ Bible Reading & Study	☐ Pastoral
☐ Children's Books	☐ Prayer & Spirituality
☐ Discipleship	☐ Resources for Children's Church
☐ Leadership	☐ Resources for Schools

Support your local bookshop
Ask about their new title information schemes.